James M'Clune

History of the Presbyterian Church in the Forks of Brandywine,

Chester County, Pa.

Brandywine Manor Presbyterian Church, from A.D. 1735 to A.D. 1885: with biographical sketches of the deceased pastors of the church.

James M'Clune

History of the Presbyterian Church in the Forks of Brandywine, Chester County, Pa.
Brandywine Manor Presbyterian Church, from A.D. 1735 to A.D. 1885: with biographical sketches of the deceased pastors of the church.

ISBN/EAN: 9783337324087

Printed in Europe, USA, Canada, Australia, Japan

Cover: Foto ©ninafisch / pixelio.de

More available books at www.hansebooks.com

HISTORY

OF THE

PRESBYTERIAN CHURCH

IN THE

FORKS OF BRANDYWINE, CHESTER COUNTY, PA.,
(BRANDYWINE MANOR PRESBYTERIAN CHURCH,)

FROM A.D. 1735 TO A.D. 1885,

WITH

BIOGRAPHICAL SKETCHES
OF
THE DECEASED PASTORS OF THE CHURCH,

AND OF THOSE WHO PREPARED FOR THE CHRISTIAN MINISTRY UNDER THE
DIRECTION OF THE REV. NATHAN GRIER.

By JAMES M'CLUNE, LL.D.,
MEMBER OF THE AMERICAN PHILOSOPHICAL SOCIETY.

"The Lord our God be with us, as He was with our fathers; let Him not leave us, nor forsake us."—1 KINGS viii. 57.

PHILADELPHIA:
PRINTED BY J. B. LIPPINCOTT COMPANY.
1885.

PREFACE.

The preparation of the following work has been delayed by the difficulty of obtaining authentic data, no regular records of the Church having been kept until a comparatively recent period. The delay, however, has enabled the writer to state some interesting facts which otherwise would have been omitted, and to continue the work to a later period. The authorities on which he has mainly relied are given at the close of each article.

For the information of those who may not have an opportunity to consult works on Ecclesiastical History, brief historical notices of the Puritans, the Huguenots, the Scotch, and the Scotch-Irish have been prefixed.

In order to prevent them from being forgotten, or to make them better known, several matters but remotely associated with religious organizations have been stated in foot-notes and appendices.

The writer thankfully acknowledges his obligations to the ministers of the Gospel and others who aided his researches and assisted him in placing on record a number of remarkable incidents connected with a "Pioneer Church" which has received many tokens of Divine guidance and approval.

J. M.

Philadelphia, June 8, 1883.

TABLE OF CONTENTS.

	PAGE
Academy, Brandywine	173
Academy, Howard	174
Academy, New London (Appendix)	232
America, discovery of	9
Bequests	198
Black, Rev. Samuel	57
Boyd, Rev. Alexander	130
Boyd, Rev. Adam	65
Buchanan, Rev. James	131
Bull, Rev. Levi, D.D.	128
Carmichael, Rev. John	79
Central Presbyterian Church, Downingtown	169
Coatesville Presbyterian Church	159
Collins, Rev. Britton E.	148
Davidson, Rev. Patrick	119
Dean, Rev. William	73
Elders, Ruling	106
Fairview Presbyterian Church	166
Graveyards	215
Grier, Rev. John F., D.D	135
Grier, Rev. John H.	140
Grier, Rev. John N. C., D.D.	99
Grier, Rev. John W.	142
Grier, Rev. Matthew B., D.D.	144
Grier, Rev. Nathan	90
Grier, Rev. Robert S.	137
Grier, Rev. Thomas	122
Happersett, Rev. Rees, D.D.	151
Heberton, Rev. William	34
Honeybrook Presbyterian Church	163
Hood, Rev. Thomas	126
Huguenots	14
Kennedy, Rev. William	134
Knight, Rev. Joshua	124

TABLE OF CONTENTS.

	PAGE
Legislators	210
Liggett, Rev. John A., D.D.	178
McCachran, Rev. Robert	145
Meeting-House, First	37
Meeting-House, Second	39
Meeting-House, Manor	41
Meeting-House, New	47
McColl, Rev. John	35
M'Conaughy, Rev. David, D.D., LL.D.	118
Moore, Rev. David W.	177
Nyce, Rev. Benjamin M.	149
Parke, Rev. Samuel	138
Parsonage	193
Pew-Holders, 1792–96	201
Physicians	211
Pinkerton, Rev. John	157
Pinkerton, Rev. William	155
Puritans	11
Quay, Rev. Anderson B.	146
Ralston, Rev. James G., D.D., LL.D.	153
Scotch and Scotch-Irish	17
Seceder Meeting-House	52
Session-Houses	196
Sextons	115
Sunday-Schools	188
Temperance Societies	204
Templeton, Rev. William H.	156
Theological Students	116
Thompson, Rev. John C.	176
Trustees	114
Umstead, Rev. Justus	152
Walker, Rev. Richard	150
Wallace, Rev. Matthew G.	121
White, Rev. Robert	132
Woods, Rev. William	117

PASTORS

OF

BRANDYWINE MANOR PRESBYTERIAN CHURCH.

FIRST PASTOR.

REV. SAMUEL BLACK, installed November, 1736; pastoral relation dissolved July, 1741.

SECOND PASTOR.

REV. ADAM BOYD (Old Side), installed August, 1741; pastoral relation ceased October, 1758.

THIRD PASTOR.

REV. WILLIAM DEAN (New Side), installed May or June, 1745; died July, 1748.

FOURTH PASTOR.

REV. JOHN CARMICHAEL, installed April, 1761; died November, 1785.

FIFTH PASTOR.

REV. NATHAN GRIER, installed August, 1787; died March, 1814.

SIXTH PASTOR.

REV. J. N. C. GRIER, D.D., installed November, 1814; resigned April, 1869.

SEVENTH PASTOR.

REV. WILLIAM W. HEBERTON, installed October, 1869; pastoral relation dissolved October, 1872.

EIGHTH PASTOR.

REV. JOHN McCOLL, installed July, 1873; present pastor.

DISCOVERY OF AMERICA.

The believer in a Superintending Providence, and especially the Christian, cannot fail to perceive the wise arrangements of Deity in the period at which America became generally known to the inhabitants of the Eastern Continent. If it had been discovered when the darkness of the Middle Ages enshrouded Europe, when the feudal system was strong in its enormity and an intolerant church held unlimited sway, superstition, oppression, and bigotry would have been increased and strengthened. The credulous monk, the lord and his vassal, and the "persecutor of heretics" would have peopled the Western shores of the Atlantic, and re-acted on a wider arena scenes which History blushes to record.

On the other hand, if this continent had not been discovered until a few centuries more had passed, thousands and tens of thousands who found refuge and a home in its wilderness solitudes would have perished by the sword or on the scaffold. The relentless cruelty of rulers and prelates would have crushed the advocates of Truth. But God in His wisdom had determined otherwise. He had decreed that the crimes of Europe should be a source of blessings to America; that those who had been subjected to fines, imprisonment, mutilation, and banishment for His name's sake should lay the foundations of a Great Republic, which would afford a home to the exile from every land and protection to men of every creed; that here a Christian nation should arise throughout whose wide domain the sound of the loom and the anvil and the hum of business would cease on every returning Sabbath,—a nation which would annually present to the world the sublime spectacle of its Chief Magistrate calling on its citizens to unite in giving thanks to Him, the Author of All Good, for blessings so freely bestowed, and so generally enjoyed.

Will it, then, be irrelevant to advert, briefly, to the history of some of those who, like Hagar, were driven by persecution into the wilderness; those whom the Angel of Mercy comforted and sustained during the whole period of Colonial weakness and despondency, and whose descendants have become more numerous than the posterity of Ishmael, but with the hand *for* not *against* every man?

Although every Protestant denomination has contributed to give tone and character to the civil and religious polity of our country, yet those to whom we as Presbyterians are chiefly indebted for liberty of conscience, for our doctrinal standards and our form of church government are the Puritans, the Huguenots, the Scotch, and the Scotch-Irish. Of these in order.

THE PURITANS.

The storm of religious persecution which swept with increasing violence over Europe during the Seventeenth Century forced thousands of her best citizens to flee to other lands. The arbitrary measures of James I. of England caused the Pilgrims to seek a refuge first in Holland and finally on the bleak shore of New England.

This colony, so feeble in the beginning, was rapidly increased by the despotic conduct of his son, Charles I., who abetted measures which the timidity of his father led that monarch to reject. The religious intolerance of Archbishop Laud, and the disturbed condition of the mother-country until Charles perished on the scaffold, added yearly to the population of the New England colonies.

But while their numbers were rapidly increasing, and they had built towns, subdued portions of the wilderness, and gathered around them the comforts of civilized life, they were not unmindful of the interests of learning and religion. In less than thirty years after the landing at Plymouth they had originated a system of public schools, established a college, now the oldest and best endowed in our country, and erected nearly fifty churches in which divine service was held every Sabbath.

During the able sway of Cromwell England enjoyed comparative quiet, and emigrants to the American colonies were few. Four years, however, had not elapsed after the death of the Great Protector before the Act of Uniformity drove upwards of two thousand Puritan clergymen from their pulpits, and placed such men as Baxter, Flaval, Howe, Allein, Calamy, Charnock, and Bunyan under the ban of ecclesiastical censure. Fines and imprisonment alike awaited the divine who proclaimed the truth and those who assembled to hear him. Under such circumstances, all that could obtain the means to do so sought a home among their brethren on this side of the Atlantic, and joyfully added to the wealth, intelligence, and prosperity of a country where there was "freedom to worship God."

These oppressive measures, which continued until the accession of the Gustavus Adolphus of England, William III., peopled the Eastern States with those who have made the sterile soil of New England a land of plenty and the fixed abode of enterprise, activity, and intelligence.

But the benefits which the first settlers of New England conferred on the land of their adoption have not been confined within its narrow limits. Wherever the descendants of the Pilgrims have found an abiding place, whether in the valleys of the Ohio, the Missouri, and the Mississippi, or on the shores of the Pacific; whether as miners, husbandmen, or manufacturers, they have carried with them their ancestral love of freedom, and their reverence for the precepts of the Bible. The printing-press, the school, and the

church have followed in the wake of their advance;
the wilderness has given place to cultivated fields, and
cities have grown with magic speed beneath their
plastic hands.

If, as Hume has observed, the precious spark of
liberty was kindled and preserved by the Puritans,—
and to them the English owe the whole freedom of
their Constitution,—the citizens of a republic which
spans a continent are indebted to those God-fearing
men and their descendants for much of the civil and
religious liberty which they enjoy.*

---

* Neal, " Hist. of the Puritans ;" Baird, " Religion in America;"
Bancroft, " Hist. of U. S. ;" Sanford, " Puritan Revolution ;" Calamy,
" Account of Ejected Ministers."

THE HUGUENOTS.

Owing to the zeal and ability of Calvin, Beza, Coligny, and their coadjutors, aided by the patronage of Margaret, Queen of Navarre, the principles of the Reformation became widely known and were eagerly embraced by many of the inhabitants of France. And although the bigoted opposition of her rulers and the fiend-like massacre of St. Bartholomew for a time diminished their number and forced many of them to obtain safety by flight, yet at the close of the sixteenth century they were sufficiently numerous and powerful to extort from Henry IV. the Edict of Nantes. This Edict guaranteed to the Protestants the free exercise of their religion. That it was often violated by the successors of Henry, even before it was formally revoked, the history of France during the Seventeenth Century fully attests. Nowhere in Europe did the spirit of religious intolerance exhibit greater malice or give rise to greater atrocities than in the persecution of the Huguenots, as the French Protestants were generally called.* Hunted like wild beasts, exposed to

---

* It is reckoned, says President Edwards, that there were martyred in this kingdom, France, for the Protestant religion, thirty-three princes, one hundred and forty-eight counts, two hundred and thirty-four barons, one hundred and forty-seven thousand gentlemen, and

ignominy, torture, and death, they were fortunate who found in foreign lands the exile which their cruel rulers sedulously endeavored to prevent. England, Holland, Switzerland, Germany, and other portions of Europe, not only afforded them an asylum, but gladly welcomed them, and those countries owe many of the mechanic arts which have increased their wealth and importance to the orderly and industrious strangers.

But the thousands of Frenchmen who were forced to abandon their native land did not find safety and a home in Europe only. A large number of them crossed the Atlantic, and sought a peaceful abiding-place among those who had planted the standard of civil and religious freedom in the Western wilderness. The colonists of New England and New York willingly received and aided them, but the milder climate of the Carolinas being more congenial to those who had been reared amid the fertile plains and vine-clad hills of France, a majority of them became citizens of what are now the Southern States. There they disseminated and practised the religious principles which had caused their exile, and contributed, by their industry, skill, and sobriety, to increase the wealth and prosperity of the country which they had made their home.

Many who have held high positions in our government, and who have discharged the duties of important trusts with uprightness and ability, could trace their lineage to the persecuted Huguenots. At the present

seven hundred and sixty thousand of the common people, all within thirty years.

time the Presbyterian churches of New England, New York, and especially of the Carolinas, number among their most useful and influential members the descendants of the countrymen of Calvin, Beza, Mornay, and Saurin.*

---

* Marsh, "Hist. of the Huguenots;" Browning, "Hist. of the Huguenots;" D'Aubigne, "Hist. of the Reformation."

THE SCOTCH AND THE SCOTCH-IRISH.

Although the Puritans and the Huguenots did much towards forming the religious character and implanting a love of liberty in the breasts of those who made America their home, they were not the only laborers in the important work. There were others who aided, by also diffusing a reverence for truth and a fear of God, the real foundations of national greatness.

The Scotch and the Scotch-Irish, as those who came from the North of Ireland were called, emigrated to this country in large numbers, bringing with them their strong attachment to learning and the doctrinal standards of the Presbyterian Church.

The Scotch had been subjected to every variety of suffering, not merely on account of their opposition to the dogmas of the Church of Rome, but because they refused to subscribe to the doctrines and forms of Episcopacy. The High Commission appointed by Charles II. exercised Inquisitorial powers, and even equalled the dread tribunals of Spain and Portugal in acts of oppression, malice, and cruelty.

In consequence of these arbitrary measures many went from Scotland to Ireland, and others sought safety on this side of the Atlantic. But it was not until the beginning of the Eighteenth Century that the Scotch and their descendants in Ireland emigrated in large numbers to America.

Driven from their homes by fanatical zeal and ecclesiastical tyranny, they naturally directed their course to the only two colonies, Maryland* and Pennsylvania, in which toleration prevailed.

In 1729, upwards of six thousand emigrants from Scotland and Ireland arrived in this State, and from that time until the middle of the century as many as twelve thousand, it is said, came over every year. A majority of them made their way into the interior, and, on account of the early frosts in the valleys and the water being less pure, they generally settled on the higher lands.

Their principal business was farming, though they were far from being skilful husbandmen. When the productiveness of the soil had been exhausted by frequent tillage, instead of resorting to fertilizers, they cleared the timber from another portion of their lands. If this resource also failed, they sought localities where the unimpaired soil of the wilderness gave a return for labor which their former possessions had ceased to afford. They therefore became the pioneers in the settlement not only of this State and of Maryland, but also of a large portion of Central Virginia and the western counties of North Carolina.

Moving in the van of civilization, with the *musket* in one hand and the *axe* in the other, they had scarcely

---

* Trinitarians only were tolerated in Maryland. No enactment abridging religious liberty has ever been placed on the statute books of Pennsylvania.

repressed Indian hostility or subdued a small part of the wilderness, when they organized the church and the school. The meeting-house was generally built of unhewn logs, and a smaller, but an equally rude, structure, served, in most instances, for a session-house and a school-house. But in these rustic church edifices men proclaimed the words of Truth whose learning and whose familiarity with the Scriptures would astonish the graduates of our theological seminaries, while the "schoolmaster from Ireland" faithfully imparted the elements of knowledge. No daily mail nor weekly newspaper kept them in communication with the rest of the world. The wilderness was their home. The broad Atlantic rolled between them and the land of their fathers. Want and danger were continually present. Nevertheless, their much-worn Bibles showed that, amid all their loneliness and privations, they sought and obtained consolation from the Holy Book which has brought joy to many a mourner and removed the shadow from many a hearth-stone.

During the struggle for National Independence, no one whose ancestry could be traced to Scotland or the North of Ireland was found among the adherents of royalty. Their patriotism and unflinching bravery were so well known that Washington, in the midnight hour of the Revolution, expressed his determination, if all other resources failed, to make his last stand among the Scotch and Scotch-Irish of the frontiers.

These races have furnished eight Chief Magistrates of the Union, twenty Governors of States, and upwards of thirty Presidents of American Colleges.

They gave us Wayne, Mercer, Montgomery, Irvine, Knox, St. Clair, Sullivan, and Morgan, of the Continental Army; the statesmen Hamilton, Madison, and Webster; the orators Patrick Henry, Calhoun, and McDuffie. To them the Presbyterian Church is indebted for the Tennents, the Blairs, the Smiths, the Allisons, Finley, Rodgers, Witherspoon, and others prominent in the annals of the struggles and the triumphs of the Church in America during the greater part of the Eighteenth Century.[*]

[*] Chambers, "Irish and Scotch-Irish Early Settlers;" Proud, "Hist. of Pennsylvania;" Gordon, "Hist. of Pennsylvania;" Hodge, "Hist. of Presbyterian Church;" Webster, "Hist. of Pres. Church."

HISTORY

OF THE

PRESBYTERIAN CHURCH

IN

"THE FORKS OF BRANDYWINE."*

THE first European settlers in what are now the Western and Central parts of Chester County were, with a few exceptions, natives of Wales. The name of a neighboring mountain and the names of several townships in this county and those adjoining would sufficiently prove this, even if history and tradition were silent.† Some of these immigrants came on account of their attachment to the principles of Penn;

---

* The term "the Forks" in early colonial annals refers not only to the point at the immediate confluence of two rivers, but to the territory included between the two streams for some miles above. Thus, "the Forks of the Delaware" comprises nearly the whole county of Northampton; "the Forks of the Susquehanna," the tract for some distance above Northumberland. (Day, "Hist. Col. Penna.") In this instance the Forks appears to have included all between the head waters of the Brandywine and the confluence of its two branches.

† Tredyffrin, Uwchlan, and Nantmeal in Chester County; Caernarvon and Brecknock, in both Berks County and Lancaster; Cymry (Cumru) in Berks County.

others, to enjoy the religious freedom accorded to all. Among them were several Presbyterian families, and as early as 1710 the records of Presbytery make mention of the church in Tredyffrin, or the Great Valley Church.

This section, however, which was known by the name of Caln,* had but few inhabitants for several years afterwards.† The first township officer, a constable, was elected in 1720. From that date, however, and especially in 1729, the Scotch and Scotch-Irish arrived and settled in considerable numbers. They were nearly all Presbyterians, or in sympathy with the Presbyterian form of church government. At first they were too few and too much scattered to organize churches, and therefore depended, for the most part, on occasional visits from the pastors of the Welsh Presbyterian churches who could address them in English.

Among those who itinerated through this section at that period, and preached in a grove or in private houses on the Sabbath, was David Evans, subsequently pastor of the church at Tredyffrin.‡

In October, 1824, the Rev. Adam Boyd was installed pastor of the churches of Octoraro (Upper

---

* It was divided into East and West Caln in 1728.
† See Appendix P.
‡ Samuel Evans, a son of David Evans, succeeded his father at Tredyffrin, but relinquished his charge without the consent of Presbytery, and was disowned by the Synod in 1751. His son Israel served as chaplain from 1777 to the close of the Revolutionary war, and died in 1807. He published several sermons. His great-grandfather was a minister in Wales.

Octoraro) and Pequea. As these were frontier churches, Mr. Boyd, in compliance with the directions of Presbytery, visited and preached in portions of the country where Presbyterians had settled, but where no church had been organized. Many of the residents of these places in time came to be regarded as members of his congregation, and contributed to his support. This appears to have been the case with those who were subsequently organized as a church in this place, for, at a meeting of the Presbytery of Donegal, held at Octoraro, June 5, 1734,* the following record was placed on the minutes: "The people at the Forks of Brandywine, being a part of Mr. Boyd's congregation, put in a supplication to the Presbytery for liberty of erecting a meeting-house for Mr. Boyd to preach in when sometimes he comes to them, which was granted."

It ought perhaps to be stated, in this connection, that the Synod or Presbytery for the limits of the authority of each were not well defined at that time, and for several years afterwards claimed and exercised the right to say where and when a meeting-house should be built. If one was erected without their consent they refused to send supplies or install a pastor; and even went so far as to censure any member of either body who conducted divine service in a building erected without their approval. A case of this kind occurred at New London, where the

---

* All dates in the last century before September, 1752, are Old Style, or eleven days earlier than they would be by the present method of reckoning time, New Style.

Presbytery ordered the doors of a meeting-house which had been built to be closed. This caused several appeals to the Synod and the Presbytery to reverse their decision, gave rise to much angry feeling, and delayed the organization of the church and the settlement of a pastor for several years. The exercise of such authority to the same extent at present would be deemed arbitrary, but then it seems to have been, and still is, in a measure, necessary, in order to prevent the erection of buildings and the organization of churches unable to support a stated ministry. But, to return to the history of this Church.

Having received permission to build a meeting-house, and, as they supposed, to organize as a distinct congregation, the members obtained a triangular lot of ground containing six and a half acres, built a house for public worship, elected elders, and applied to Presbytery at its meeting in April (4), 1735, held at Chestnut Level, for supplies. At the same time an application was made by the congregation of Octoraro "desiring the subscription of these people (those in the Forks of Brandywine) may be continued for Mr. Boyd's support." The Presbytery, after hearing the statements of the parties, came to the following, among other, conclusions:

"First. That the said people (the people in the Forks) had quite mistaken the matter in deeming themselves already erected, whereas it is not so; only they were granted leave to build an house for their more convenient enjoying the visits of Mr. Boyd."

"Secondly. The Presbytery judge that said people be contented as part of Mr. Boyd's charge as formerly;

and, further, Presbytery judge that said people have acted ungratefully towards Mr. Boyd and the congregation of Octoraro for his former kindness and care toward them."

The Presbytery also ordered them to make a "list of all the people of our communion or profession dwelling in the confines of said designed erection next to the border of Octoraro, and send said list to Mr. Boyd."

At a meeting of the Presbytery of Donegal, held June 10, 1735, Jno. Hamilton, as commissioner from the Forks of Brandywine, presented a "supplication" to be erected into a distinct congregation, a list of the people according to the order of Presbytery, and a paper, unsubscribed, alleged to be from said people, casting groundless reflections on Mr. Boyd. "With this paper the Presbytery find great fault."

The Presbytery ordered the usual perambulations, and also selected two persons, who were directed to choose a third, to act as arbitrators in settling the difficulty with William Craige, "who complained of being wronged in relation to his interest in a part of the meeting-house."

On the 15th of September, 1735,[*] another "supplication" from the Forks of Brandywine was presented to the Presbytery, and also a request that Presbytery would concur with them in endeavoring to procure a visit from some of the young gentlemen lately arrived from Ireland and connected with New Castle Presbytery, in order to give such visitor a call.

---

[*] 26th of September, New Style.

The Presbytery, after observing that they had been badly treated, and having received an apology from the Commissioners for their "misdemeanor," and an assurance that all arrearages to Mr. Boyd would be paid until the next November, "erected said people into a *distinct congregation.*"

The Presbytery also complained of the location of the meeting-house, and recommended that no dead be buried there until the matter was finally settled.

In April, 1736, Jno. Hamilton and James Ward appeared as Commissioners from the Forks of Brandywine, with a list of subscriptions and a call to Mr. Samuel Black, one of the young men above referred to. The Presbytery did not consider the call to be in proper form, and also disapproved of the sum of fifty pounds mentioned in the call, when the subscription was nearly sixty-six, but placed the consideration of it with Mr. Black.

May 23, 1736, at a meeting of the Presbytery held at Nottingham, Robert Hamilton and Edward Irwin, Commissioners from the Forks of Brandywine, presented a call to Mr. Black, with the amount increased to fifty-five pounds Pennsylvania currency ($146⅔). "The call was placed in the hands of Mr. Black, and he accepted it."

On the 10th of November, 1736, the Presbytery met at the Forks of Brandywine, and ordained and installed Mr. Black as pastor of the congregation.

No records remain of the number of members of the Church when Mr. Black became pastor. Nor are there any means of ascertaining the attendance on the Sabbath, or the interest manifested in the subject of religion. That the members were few, and the weekly assemblages far from large, may be inferred from the condition of the country, which was still, to a great extent, a wilderness. This is shown by the report of the Commissioners who laid out the Paxtang Road* in 1735-36. In that report they make no mention of farms or buildings of any kind, except the "Presbyterian's Meeting-House," in the entire distance from the Welsh Mountain, or Lancaster County line, to several miles northeast of this place.

Indeed, even so late as the close of the Revolutionary war, the roads were little more than "bridle-paths" through the forest. Those, therefore, whom business detained to a late hour at Chester, then the "seat of justice," were often obliged to leave the "finding of the way home" to that sagacious animal, the horse.

Mr. Black had been settled but a short time as pastor, when the difference of views which prevailed in the Presbyterian Church, and which finally led to the "Great Schism," caused dissensions between him and his people, and gave rise to charges and counter-charges which were far from creditable to either the pastor or the members of his flock. This state of affairs, alike unfavorable to the growth of the Church and the promotion of piety, continued in this and other congregations until the Protest of June 1, 1741, closed the controversy, and the Presbyterian

---

* Peixtan, spelled Peichong, Pechetan, Paxtang, and Paxton, in old records, once an Indian wigwam or village where Harrisburg now stands. (Rupp, "Hist. of Lancaster Co.")

Church became two separate bodies with a distinct organization.

Immediately after this event a majority of Mr. Black's charge withdrew, and, those who remained being too few to sustain weekly services on the Sabbath, the pastoral relation was dissolved.

The minority, Old Side, either by an amicable arrangement or a determined resistance, kept possession of the meeting-house and ground, and obtained permission from Presbytery to engage the services of Mr. Boyd, of Octoraro, one-half of his time, at a yearly salary of twenty pounds, Pennsylvania currency.

Mr. Boyd was installed on the 12th of August, 1741, and continued to be their pastor until a few months after the reunion, May 28, 1758, when he ceased to occupy their pulpit, although the pastoral relation was not formally dissolved.

In the mean time, those who seceded, New Side, were not inactive. They purchased a rectangular lot of ground containing three acres, a little to the east of the former church property, and erected a comfortable building for public worship. They were regularly supplied by the Synod of New Brunswick until May or June, 1745, when the Rev. Mr. Dean became their pastor. He remained until his death, in July, 1748.

Of the condition of this church during his short ministry no record can be found,* but, from the tra-

---

* The Minutes of the "New Side" Presbytery of New Castle are lost.

ditional popularity and faithfulness of Mr. Dean, the conclusion may be drawn that it was highly prosperous.

After his death, although the congregation gave a call to a Mr. John Todd, and perhaps to some others, they remained without a stated pastor, but, as the heat of the controversy cooled with the lapse of years, many of them attended the ministry of Mr. Boyd.

From the withdrawal of Mr. Boyd, in the autumn of 1758, until the installation of Mr. Carmichael, in the spring of 1761, the pulpits of both the churches were vacant, and public worship seems to have been in a measure suspended.

After the settlement of Mr. Carmichael, an almost immediate change took place. Energetic, zealous, and faithful, he soon acquired a commanding influence, which resulted in the erection of a large and convenient meeting-house, the restoration of harmony among the people, and the addition of many to the congregation.

During the struggle for National Independence, when, as happens in almost all wars, inroads are made on morals and piety languishes, the religious fervor of his people was not permitted to cool, nor the efforts to arrest the torrent of vice to become either few or weak.

Believing with the Hebrew King, that he who winneth souls is wise, Mr. Carmichael, after the close of the Revolutionary conflict, labored with increased diligence for the conversion of sinners, until his death left his congregation to mourn the loss of their beloved pastor.

From the commencement to the end of his ministry, although there were few copious showers, yet the outspread fleece was always wet with the dews of heaven.

A few months after the decease of Mr. Carmichael the church building was destroyed by fire. As this occurred at a period of financial depression and uncertainty, the hand of affliction seemed to be laid heavily upon the flock without a shepherd. Trusting, however, that the Great Head of the Church would temper His chastisements with mercy, they obtained supplies from the Presbytery of New Castle and also of Philadelphia, engaged energetically in the collection of funds, and soon commenced the reconstruction of their meeting-house.

Among those who supplied the vacant pulpit, was Nathan Grier, a licentiate of the Presbytery of Philadelphia. His preaching was so well received that before the building was completed the congregation gave him a unanimous call. This he accepted, and, having placed himself under the care of the Presbytery of New Castle, to which the church belonged, was ordained and installed the twenty-second of August, 1787.

Mr. Grier entered with zeal on the discharge of the duties of his pastorate, and the results of his industry and faithfulness soon became manifest. The rebuilding of the meeting-house was finished. The difficulties which arose from the unsettled monetary condition of the country were overcome, and the burden of sorrow was lifted from the hearts of those who, adopting the plaintive language of the prophet,* had refused to be comforted on account of the destruction of the house of God and the death of him who had ministered at its altar.

Having the reputation of an able divine, "apt to teach," members of his congregation and others who were preparing for the Christian ministry gladly placed themselves under his direction. They were faithfully trained, and near a score of young men went forth prepared to battle with the arch-enemy of souls.

But the labors of Mr. Grier as a teacher and a pastor were unexpectedly ended. While his eye was scarcely dimmed and his natural force unabated, he was removed from his abode on earth to his Heavenly home. The grief on account of his death was widespread, and a greater number followed his remains to the grave than the most aged had ever seen assembled on a similar occasion.

How many were connected with the Church at the commencement of the ministry of the Rev. Nathan Grier cannot be ascertained. At its close the number of members was two hundred and thirty-two. A record of those admitted annually to the Church the last ten years of his pastorate has been preserved. Taking the addition to the membership each year of that period as the annual average, not less than six hundred became connected with the Church during the nearly twenty-seven years of his ministry.

Shortly after the death of Mr. Grier, a call from

---

* Isaiah lxiv. 11.

the congregation was placed in the hands of his younger son, the Rev. J. N. C. Grier. This call he accepted, and on the twenty-fourth of November, 1814, entered on his pastorate of upwards of fifty-four years.

At that period many of the customs and habits of the first settlers prevailed. The members of the congregation came on horseback or a-foot to attend the services of the sanctuary, a large number of them clothed in garments of domestic manufacture. Visits to the cities, or intercourse with the world at a distance, were limited. There was no post-office nearer than Coatesville or Downingtown, and few religious periodicals. Sunday-schools were not organized in a single church connected with the Presbytery, and societies for the suppression of intemperance were unknown. But an increase of facilities for travel and the general advance of improvement wrought changes. A post-office was established at a convenient distance in 1816. A Sunday-school was organized in 1820, a missionary society in 1829, and a temperance association formed in 1831. A religious newspaper, published at Wilmington, Delaware, was taken by several members of the Church, and the taste for reading created among the young by the publications of the Sunday-School and the Tract Society* led, a few years later, to the general support and perusal of the *Presbyterian, Presbyterian Journal, American Messenger,* and other religious periodicals.

In several of these movements Dr. Grier took an

---

* Organized in 1825.

active and in others a leading part, while all of them had his cordial support.

But his labors were not confined to merely bettering the temporal condition, or in improving and increasing the facilities for acquiring knowledge. In the pulpit he faithfully preached Jesus Christ and Him crucified as the sinner's only hope of safety, and earnestly besought the impenitent to lay hold of the salvation offered in the Gospel. At every communion there was an addition to the church membership, but in 1822, and especially in 1831 and several years immediately following, there was a copious "refreshing from the Lord," and a large number became members of his charge. Such was the success of his labors that, notwithstanding four Presbyterian Churches which "live and flourish," and ten belonging to other denominations were organized within what had been the bounds of his charge, the membership of the Church at the close of his ministry was about the same as when he entered on the discharge of his duties as pastor.

Although Dr. Grier was not called upon, as Mr. Carmichael had been, to aid in the struggle for National Independence, nor, like his father, to train young men as ambassadors for Christ, yet he added by his faithfulness to the number of those who went forth as heralds of the everlasting Gospel. During his pastorate sixteen young men to whom he first broke the "Bread of Life" devoted themselves to the Christian ministry. Two of them, Mr. David Templeton and Mr. Matthew Brown, were removed to the "better land" before they had finished their theological course. The other fourteen, of whom short biographical sketches are given in this work, became faithful soldiers of the Cross. Eight of them have fought the good fight and finished their course rejoicing. One, after a successful pastorate of twenty-one years, was forced by ill health to withdraw from active service at the altar; another was the founder and for a long period the principal of a popular educational institution, and a third is the senior editor of a widely-circulated and influential religious newspaper. The remaining five are engaged in making known "the unsearchable riches of Christ" in each of the Middle and one of the Western States.

But while Dr. Grier was zealously and earnestly engaged in the discharge of the duties of his sacred calling, the lapse of more than half a century brought changes. The members of Presbytery with whom he first met had passed away. A majority of his hearers on the Sabbath were the descendants of those who had invited him to take the spiritual oversight of the congregation. The infirmities of more than threescore and ten pressed heavily upon him, and, feeling that he was no longer able to labor in the Master's vineyard, he requested and obtained a dissolution of the pastoral relation.*

After the retirement of Dr. Grier the congregation was dependent on supplies. Among those who occupied the vacant pulpit was the Rev. Wm. W. Heberton, a licentiate of the Central Presbytery of Philadelphia. The services of Mr. Heberton were

* Appendix II.

so well received that a call made on the 18th of July, 1869, by the congregation, to become their pastor, was placed in his hands, which he accepted, and was ordained and installed October 28, 1869. The pastoral relation was dissolved in October, 1872, by the Presbytery of Chester.

During the ministry of Mr. Heberton the parsonage was built, twenty-nine were added to the membership of the Church, and three of the Ruling Elders were removed by death.

In June, 1873, Mr. Heberton was installed pastor of the Presbyterian Church at Elkton, Md., where "the work of the Lord has prospered in his hands." Near a hundred have united with the Church during his ministry, Christian harmony prevails, and the influence for good of both the pastor and his people is daily increasing.*

After the withdrawal of Mr. Heberton the pulpit was supplied by the Rev. Mr. Bingham, of Oxford, Pa., and by some young men who were candidates for settlement. Among them was the Rev. John M'Coll, a graduate of the University of Toronto, Canada, and of the Theological Seminary at Princeton.

---

* Mr. Heberton is a native of Columbia County, in this State. His classical studies were pursued at Media, Delaware County, and his collegiate at Lafayette, Easton, where he was graduated in 1865. He spent the next eighteen months after his graduation in the study of medicine, and then entered the Theological Seminary at Princeton. He finished his preparation for the ministry in the spring of 1869, and was licensed in April of that year. His pastoral oversight of this congregation was his first charge.

The ministrations of Mr. M'Coll were so satisfactory that he received a call from the congregation to become their pastor, and was ordained and installed by a committee of the Presbytery of Chester on the 24th of July, 1873. On that occasion the Rev. J. Collier presided, Rev. Mr. Totheroth preached the sermon, Rev. Mr. Pomeroy charged the pastor, and Rev. Mr. Collier the people. The trial-sermon of Mr. M'Coll was from Heb. iv. 12.

The ministry of Mr. M'Coll has been successful, and the membership of the church under his discreet oversight has increased. Two Sabbath-schools have been organized in the outlying districts of his charge. The new church edifice is filled on the Sabbath, and a growing interest in the subject of religion is daily becoming more manifest.

The meeting-house having become scarcely safe for public worship and the congregation having resolved to build another, Mr. M'Coll aided greatly in the furtherance of the work by the collection and disbursement of funds, the arrangement of plans, and encouragement at periods of difficulty and despondency. Finally, his efforts, seconded by the liberality of his congregation, were crowned with success. When the new meeting-house, free from debt, was dedicated to the service of the Triune God, he could thankfully and reverently have asked, in the words of the Psalmist, "Who am I and what is my people that we should be able to offer so willingly after this sort?"

May the pastorate so auspiciously begun be long continued, and on the Great Day may many, very many, whom he had gathered into the fold of the

Redeemer, shine as stars in the "Crown of his rejoicing."*

MEETING-HOUSES.†

FIRST MEETING-HOUSE.

Of this building we have no authentic information, except such as some remains of the foundation which existed at a comparatively recent period afforded of its size and situation, and a few collateral statements which have escaped the ravages of time. In all else tradition is the only authority. But in this instance tradition agrees with the recorded description of buildings erected for the same purpose in the pioneer settlements of Virginia, North Carolina, and the western counties of our own State.

This meeting-house, which was built either in the summer or fall of 1734, stood in what is now a part of the "upper graveyard," a few rods east from the northwest corner of the ground which the congregation had obtained for church purposes. The size was about forty feet by twenty-five. It was placed, like nearly all buildings erected at that period, with the front to the south, and north of the Indian trail, then used as the highway. The material used was un-

---

* Minutes of Presbytery of Newcastle; Minutes of Presbytery of Donegal; Dr. Grier's "Historical Discourse;" Church Records; Local Memoranda.

† Buildings set apart for public worship by the early settlers, Baptists, Presbyterians, and Friends, were called meeting-houses, as they still are by the last-named denomination. In England the places of worship of the Dissenters are uniformly called meeting-houses.

hewn logs, ridged and notched at the corners, and let into what workmen call a king-post in the middle of each side. It was low, dimly lighted, unplastered, and without any means of obtaining heat. Logs cleft in two and smoothed on one side served as seats, and the pulpit was little more than a rough, elevated table. Rudely constructed and poorly furnished, it was also far from being a substantial building. This is shown by the fact that, although it was used, at least twice a month, during twenty-five years for divine worship, and considerable repairs must have been made, yet at the end of that period it was wholly unfit for the public services of the sanctuary.

That comfortless structure would contrast strangely with the commodious edifice which has recently been built; and yet many interesting events, events which ought never to be forgotten, are associated with that primitive meeting-house. In it those worshipped who organized a church in this portion of what was then a wilderness. There Samuel Black entered on the arduous labors of a pioneer minister of the Gospel; and there Adam Boyd, during seventeen years, broke the Bread of Life to those who had come for Spiritual nourishment through pathless forests and from humble homes, and who devoutly thanked God that they could worship Him without the dread of banishment, the dungeon, or the stake.

More than a century has passed since Black and Boyd were called to their reward, and the features of all and even the names of the greater part of their hearers are no longer remembered; but the germs of truth which they planted continue to flourish and bear immortal fruit. The ground which they devoted to sacred purposes is still hallowed ground, and along the course of one hundred and fifty years are strewn blessed proofs that the Most High has had the Church then organized in His Holy Keeping.

SECOND MEETING-HOUSE.

This was probably built in 1744, and may have been one of the inducements which led the Rev. Mr. Dean to accept a second call from the New Side congregation. It stood on the vacant ground immediately above the "lower graveyard," with the front to the south. It was a well-constructed frame building, about forty-five feet by thirty-five, one story high, with a hipped or angular roof, and without a gallery.*

There does not appear to have been any means for affording heat in the building; but this inconvenience was probably obviated, to some extent, by the Session-House, which was placed near the southeast corner of the property. This, like the Session-Houses built at an early period in other parts of this State, may have been furnished with a fireplace, where persons could have the benefit of heat before they entered the main building.

When the union of the Presbyterian Church took place, in 1758, and the first meeting-house was aban-

---

* The difference between the first and the second meeting-house shows the advance which had been made in ten years in the preparation and use of materials. The first saw-mill in the vicinity, according to tradition, was built about 1740, on the West Branch of the Brandywine, above the Beaver Dam.

doned, this building was too small to accommodate all who assembled on the Sabbath, and after the erection of the Manor Meeting-House it was no longer used as a place for public worship. It remained unoccupied several years, until the members who resided in the eastern bounds of the congregation moved it to the ground connected with the new church edifice and placed it about sixty yards to the east of that building. There it served, partly as a shed for standing horses, partly as a place for depositing saddles and umbrellas in stormy weather, and remained until the winter of 1812 or '13, when it was blown down and the materials used for fuel.

Although this building stood upwards of two-thirds of a century, public worship was not conducted in it more than fifteen or sixteen years; but during those years many incidents worthy of record took place within its walls. In it Dean performed his last labor ere he was called to his Heavenly rest; and Samuel Blair, John Blair, William Tennent, and others scarcely less eminent, dwelt with awakening earnestness on the condition of the lost. There John Carmichael was installed as pastor of the united congregations, and entered on that important relation which ended only with his life, and from its sacred desk was diffused a warm, active piety, alike opposed to cold formality and a listless profession.

THIRD MEETING-HOUSE.—"MANOR MEETING-HOUSE."*

The erection of this meeting-house, as is stated elsewhere, was due in a great measure to the energy and popularity of the pastor, Mr. Carmichael. The united congregations rightly judging that the number attending on the services of the sanctuary would be largely increased, determined to erect a building which would accommodate all. They immediately made efforts to obtain the means, and were so successful that the work was commenced in the latter part of the summer of 1761. Their recently installed pastor, whose labor in forwarding the undertaking had been unceasing, delivered an animated address when the corner-stone was laid, and at the conclusion of the ceremonies, in accordance with the custom of the time, threw a Twenty-Shilling note on the stone to treat the masons. The building was erected under the direction of Samuel Cunningham,† chief carpenter. No cut stone

---

* It received the name of the Manor Meeting-House because it was placed within the limits of Springtown (Springton) Manor. This Manor was laid out in 1729, but its boundaries were not finally determined until near a score of years afterwards. It included nearly the whole of the present Township of Wallace, and portions of West Brandywine, West Nantmeal, and Honeybrook. The first settlers in this Manor were, with two or three exceptions, Scotch and Scotch-Irish. The misnomer, Brandywine Manor, given to the first post-office established near the Church edifice, gradually led to its being applied to the Church itself, by which name, except in ecclesiastical records, it is now generally known.

† Samuel Cunningham, whose remains were interred in the "lower graveyard," was a Member of the Assembly from Chester County in 1776–77 ; a Delegate to the Convention which formed the First Constitution of Pennsylvania ; a Collector of the Excise, and many

was used in the construction, nor any lumber which was not obtained from the neighboring forests, except the outer covering of the roof.

This Meeting-House was sixty-five feet by forty-five, two stories high, and at the time of its erection was the largest stone edifice in the northwestern part of Chester County.

The Pulpit was placed in the South side of the building. There was an entrance at the East end, and another at the West, connected by an aisle which equally divided the lower part of the building or audience-room. Another aisle led from this to an entrance on the North side opposite the Pulpit. All the pews were arranged from North to South. Those, therefore, who occupied the pews North of the main aisle sat with a side to the Pulpit. There were no flues nor any arrangement made in the construction of the building for supplying heat.

This Meeting-House was never completed according to the original plan; the gallery and some other parts being omitted on account of a want of funds.

In order to afford some degree of warmth vessels made of sheet-iron and shaped like a mill-hopper were placed in the aisles and filled with live coals. Some of the coals falling on the floor caused the destruction of the building in February, 1786. The sexton, it was said, saw the light when the fire might have been extinguished, but being a believer in ap-

---

years a Justice of the Peace. His death occurred June 22, 1806, aged seventy-four. A great-grandson of Esqr. Cunningham, Matthew Brown, died while preparing to enter the ministry.

paritions, he did not venture near until others attracted by the light arrived, when nothing could be done to arrest the progress of the flames.

The members of the congregation, deeply grieved by the recent death of their beloved pastor, Mr. Carmichael, were now subjected to the additional affliction of seeing all that was combustible in their Meeting-House reduced to ashes. They were dismayed but not disheartened. In the beginning of the next month, March, 1786, they addressed a well-written and earnest appeal* to their Christian brethren for assistance, and appointed agents to solicit aid.

Among the most diligent of those engaged in collecting funds was Elder William Hunter. He called for that purpose not only at every house within a distance of several miles, but even accosted persons on the highway, earnestly requesting and thankfully receiving even the smallest amount. He also visited Chester, the Turk's Head, now West Chester, and Philadelphia, then the seat of the general government, where he obtained assistance from the following well-known citizens:

Dr. Rush and Dr. Franklin, Signers of the Declaration of Independence.

David Rittenhouse, the celebrated mathematician, and the first Director of the Mint of the United States.

Edward Shippen, the first Mayor of Philadelphia, and Chief Justice of the Supreme Court of this State.

William Shippen, a Professor in the University of

---

* See Appendix A.

Pennsylvania, and the first who delivered a course of Medical Lectures in America.

William Bradford, Attorney-General of the United States.

Colonel Andrew Porter, an officer in the army of the Revolution, and Surveyor-General of Pennsylvania.

Tench Coxe, an able writer on Political Economy.

General John Potter, a distinguished officer in the Continental army.

John Nicholson, the well-known land agent.

Jonathan D. Sargent, at that time the leading member of the Philadelphia Bar.

Mark Wilcox, an influential merchant.

Joseph and Colonel William Dean, sons of the Rev. William Dean, and many others less known, but not less benevolent.

These names are given to show that at a period when the country was impoverished by war, when it had only a depreciated and depreciating currency, and was without a stable form of government, men of all classes contributed to the fund for the restoration of the venerable building which withstood the storms of more than a century and around which so many hallowed associations clustered.

But to return to the history of the reconstruction of the Church edifice. When sufficient funds had been collected, as the members of the congregation supposed, to restore their Meeting-House, the work was commenced. The walls, with the exception of the gables, having been found on examination to be so far uninjured as not to require them to be taken down, the reconstruction was confined mainly to roofing the building and restoring the interior. In doing this several alterations and some additions were made. A gallery was placed along each end and the side opposite the Pulpit. The pews North of the Main Aisle, which formerly ran from North to South, were arranged in a direction East and West, or at right angles to those South of that avenue. Flues were built in the gables, and ten-plate stoves, the gift of Colonel Grubb, of Lancaster County, were placed in the aisles. The Pulpit was remodelled, made to occupy less space, and furnished with a "sounding-board," or projection from the wall over the head of the speaker. At the base of the Pulpit and not unlike it, though smaller, a stand was arranged for the use of the precentors, or those who led the choir. To prevent accidents by fire in the same manner as had occurred, the aisles were laid with mortar or cement instead of boards.

The reconstruction was done under the direction of Samuel Cunningham, Esq., who, as before stated, had the oversight of the building when it was first erected.*
Although the work was commenced in the summer of 1786, it progressed slowly, and the building was not entirely completed when the Rev. Nathan Grier was installed as pastor, in August, 1787. The cost, as appears by the Treasurer's account, was a little more than a Thousand Pounds Pennsylvania currency, or about twenty-seven hundred dollars.

* He superintended the erection of the second Meeting-House at Fagg's Manor, and probably of the third Meeting-House at Octoraro, built in 1769.

This meeting-house remained without any change in the interior and with trifling repairs, except a new roof (in 1827), until 1839. In that year it was remodelled and made to conform in a considerable degree to the plan adopted in the arrangement of Church edifices at the present time. As the alterations then made remained until the building was taken down, in 1875, it is unnecessary to state them except as matters of record. Suffice it to say that the door at the North side, and also the one at the East end, were walled up. Instead of these a door was made on the South side about twelve feet from the East corner. An aisle led from this door in front of the Pulpit, which was placed in a recess at the East end of the building. A gallery was constructed along both sides and the end opposite the Pulpit. This gallery was reached by a flight of stairs on each side of the vestibule, which adjoined the main entrance at the West end. Aisles with a row of pews on each side led from the vestibule to the aisle in front of the Pulpit.

Such are the main facts connected with a building whose walls stood one hundred and fourteen years, and whose size and situation remained unchanged during that long period. When it was erected there was no other house for public worship within ten miles in any direction except the Seceder Meeting-House, no longer in existence, and the Friends' Meeting-House "up on the hill from the valley," Old Calu, built in 1756. Now, in addition to four other Church edifices belonging to Presbyterians, there are in the same bounds twenty buildings for Divine worship, occupied by five different denominations.

It may be stated as a fitting close to the history of the Manor Meeting-House, that from the dedication of the building in 1761 until it was taken down in 1875,* the congregations worshipping in it were not more than three years without a stated ministry. Also that during one hundred and five years of that interval its pulpit was occupied by three pastors only, —the Rev. John Carmichael, the Rev. Nathan Grier, and the Rev. J. N. C. Grier, D.D. An example of Christian harmony and of attachment between pastors and people which has few parallels even in the annals of the Presbyterian Church.†

FOURTH MEETING-HOUSE.

The Manor Meeting-House having become in a measure unsafe, and in need of extensive repairs, the question arose, whether it would be better to place that building in a proper condition for public worship or to erect another. On the one hand, it was evident that repairing it would only be a postponement for some years of the erection of a church edifice, and that, if refitted in the best manner possible, it would still be wanting in a lecture-room and other conveniences, now deemed necessary in houses set apart for the services of the sanctuary. On the other hand, the expense of erecting a building at a period of pecuniary embarrassment, and the desire of many to preserve

---

* The last sermon was preached in the building June 13, 1875, by the pastor, Mr. M'Coll, from Jeremiah vi. 13.
† Local Memoranda; Records of Session; Minutes of Presbytery of Newcastle.

the meeting-house in which they and their fathers had worshipped, were subjects for earnest and thoughtful consideration.

Several meetings were held, at which the matter was discussed and carefully examined in all its bearings, but without arriving at a definite conclusion. At last a committee was appointed to report on the condition of the meeting-house, and to state whether it would be best to repair or to build.

On the 24th of March, 1874, the committee reported that after hearing the opinion of competent men, Messrs. Sloan and Bunn, of Honey Brook, who had examined the meeting-house, it had been unanimously resolved to recommend the erection of a new church edifice. The report was accepted, and a resolution adopted to proceed as soon as possible in constructing a building. The pastor, Mr. McColl, was appointed to solicit funds for that purpose, and requested to report when, according to his judgment, an amount sufficient to warrant a commencement of the work had been secured.

Having entered on the performance of the task assigned him with ancestral Scotch zeal and perseverance, Mr. McColl was able to state at a meeting of the congregation, held the next September (15th), that in addition to many offers of labor gratuitously, upwards of ten thousand dollars had been subscribed. It was therefore determined to commence the work early the next spring. At the same meeting Messrs. John Ralston, William Templeton, and Baxter B. McClure were chosen a committee to procure plans and have the general oversight in the construction of the building. Mr. McColl was also appointed treasurer of the funds collected for the "new erection."

The members of the committee, in compliance with their instructions, examined several church edifices, and engaged Mr. Samuel Sloan, an architect of Philadelphia, to furnish plans. They likewise invited proposals from builders, and, after careful deliberation, awarded the contract for the greater portion of the work to Mr. William Poole, of Philadelphia.

The masons began work on the foundation the 28th of June, 1875, and the corner-stone was laid with appropriate ceremonies* on the 7th of August in the same year. Owing, however, to unfavorable weather, the limited means of the contractor, and other causes, the work progressed slowly, and in the beginning of July, 1876, after all the stone had been laid, Mr. Poole abandoned the contract. The members of the committee were therefore obliged to take upon themselves the completing of the building. They employed Ulysses K. Beam, who superintended the carpenter work, Samuel B. Buchannan the plastering, and S. B. Williams the painting.

The building, with the exception of a part of the tower and the spire, having been at last finished, the 14th of December, 1876, was appointed for the dedication of it to the service of Almighty God.

On that occasion Dr. J. N. C. Grier made the opening prayer, Dr. Matthew B. Grier read a portion of Scripture, Dr. N. G. Parke, of Pittston, Pa., led in prayer, and Dr. Dickey, pastor of the Calvary

---

* See Appendix B.

Church, Philadelphia, preached the sermon from II. Cor. iii. 18. Remarks were also made by Rev. J. C. Thompson, then of Hagerstown, Md., Rev. J. A. Liggett, of Rahway, N. J., Rev. Thomas S. Long, of Bloomsbury, in the same State, and Rev. David W. Moore, at that time a resident of McVeytown, Pa.

As a considerable amount was still needed to pay the indebtedness, after the close of the religious exercises an effort was made to procure funds sufficient for that purpose. When about three thousand six hundred dollars had been subscribed, it was concluded to postpone the dedication until the next Sabbath, in order that the building might, if possible, be consecrated to the service of the Most High free from encumbrance.

On Sabbath, December 17, after a sermon by the Rev. J. C. Thompson, and addresses by the Rev. David W. Moore and the pastor, the amount needed to pay all arrearages was pledged. The dedicatory prayer was then offered by the Rev. Mr. Moore, and the congregation, after singing the 137th Psalm, was dismissed, rejoicing.

The building thus happily completed and freed from debt stands a short distance south of the site occupied by the Manor Meeting-House, with the front towards the North and parallel to the public road. It is seventy-three feet by fifty-four feet, with a recess for the pulpit, and contains a lecture- and Sabbath-school-rooms below, and an audience-room, with a gallery at one end, above. The audience-room is sixty-eight feet by forty-nine including gallery, with a height of thirty-seven feet to the apex in the centre. This room is neatly and appropriately furnished, and the pews, which afford seats for about four hundred and fifty, are convenient and well arranged.

A striking feature, and one which adds beauty and interest to the building, is the memorial windows. Of these, there are no less than nine commemorative of the Rev'ds John Carmichael, Nathan Grier, and J. N. C. Grier, D.D., Elder James Ralston, Elder James K. Grier, Joseph Mackelduff, Benjamin and Agnes McClure, the Manor Sunday-School and the Sunday-School at Rockville.

The entire structure presents an imposing appearance, and, owing to the elevated situation, is visible at a distance of several miles in almost every direction.

The cost of the building and improvement of the enclosure may be placed at twenty-one thousand dollars. Of this, about one thousand dollars was contributed in labor. The ladies of the congregation raised nearly fourteen hundred dollars by festivals, a fair, and a supper. The memorial windows were presented by the members of the Sunday-Schools and by the friends or relatives of the godly persons whose names they are intended to perpetuate.

Although great credit should be given to the members of the Building Committee for the careful manner in which they performed the duty assigned them, and also to those who so liberally contributed funds for the erection of the building, yet much is due to the popularity, zeal, and perseverance of the pastor, Mr. McColl. Like his predecessor, Mr. Carmichael, he has been instrumental in obtaining the construction of a large and substantial building for public worship, which will remain long after he has been removed to a " house not made with hands."

Such is a brief history of the Fourth Meeting-House. What the record will be when it shall have been so much impaired by the destroying hand of time as to require another in its stead, is known only to Him "who sees the end from the beginning." But trusting that He will watch over and bless the Church established in this place, in the future as He has done in the past, may it not be hoped that those who assemble the last time within this consecrated building will be able truthfully to say, 'Here the Gospel has been preached with faithfulness and power. Here many have been brought to a knowledge of the Saviour. From these hallowed precincts an influence has been diffused whose beneficial results will never be fully known until the "Book of Remembrance" shall be opened, and all the descendants of Adam shall stand before their Final Judge.'*

SECEDER MEETING-HOUSE.

Messrs. Gellatly† and Arnott, the first missionaries sent by the Seceder Church to America, arrived in 1753. Being energetic, faithful, and well received, especially by those of the early settlers who had been connected with that denomination in the fatherland, and favored by the schism in the Presbyterian Church, they, Henderson, Mason, Annan, Smart, and others,

---

* Minutes of Building Committee; Records of Session; Com. from the Pastor, Mr. McColl; Local Memoranda.

† Gellatly died in April (12th), 1761.

gathered congregations and erected buildings for public worship. One of these was placed on the southern slope of the Barren Hill, where the Wagontown Road intersects the road leading to Coatesville, and a few hundred yards from two Presbyterian Meeting-Houses. This building, erected in 1756 or '57, was poorly constructed, and had become so much out of repair in 1780 that a board tent was placed in front of it and used in its stead. Religious exercises were conducted in the tent by men of learning and ability until about the beginning of the present century, when the older members being dead and others having connected themselves with the Manor Presbyterian Church, those who remained were too few to support a stated ministry, and finally ceased to be a distinct organization. As a consequence the buildings were neglected and soon decayed. Owing to its being used as a school-house, and receiving some repairs, the Session-house, which was built of very small logs, remained a few years after the other structures were in ruins. No traces either of it or of the Church edifice and tent are visible.

The graveyard, which occupies about one-eighth of an acre, is kept in repair by some of the descendants of those who obtained the site, and is still used as a burial-ground. It contains a number of graves, many of them unmarked. The first memorial stone placed in it bears the date of 1768, the last of 1880.

John Gilleland, who owned the adjoining farm, probably gave the land occupied by the buildings and graveyard. His only son, who was murdered by some Hessian marauders shortly after the battle of

Brandywine, was laid to rest in this enclosure, but no lettered stone preserves the name of the victim of hireling barbarity. A grandson of Mr. Gilleland, the Rev. James Buchanan, was long a faithful minister of the Presbyterian Church. Nathaniel Erwin, a soldier of the Continental army and a son of one of the first settlers, and several of his descendants, are buried in this graveyard.

While the futility of attempting to support three churches, differing in non-essentials only, within a short distance of one another, is shown by their becoming merged in one, it nevertheless makes manifest the determination of our fathers to sustain a preached Gospel, and their adherence to the doctrines and modes of worship which they had learned and practised before their settlement in the wilds of America.*

---

* McKerrow, "Hist. of Secession Church;" Buck, "Theological Dictionary;" "Reminiscences of James Dorlan;" Local Memoranda.

BIOGRAPHICAL SKETCHES.

BIOGRAPHICAL SKETCHES

OF THE

DECEASED PASTORS OF BRANDYWINE MANOR PRESBYTERIAN CHURCH.

"And I will give you pastors according to mine heart, which shall feed you with knowledge and understanding."—JER. iii. 15.

REV. SAMUEL BLACK.

Born 1700.   Died 1770.

As has been already stated, the pulpits of the Presbyterian Church, during the first half-century of its existence in America, were mainly supplied by natives of Scotland and the North of Ireland. Some of them came in answer to the Macedonian cry, "come over and help us," others actuated by the spirit which guided Martyn, Heber, Birney, and their fellow-laborers to the inhospitable regions of Asia and Africa. They were mostly young men, who left home and its comforts to share the privations and promote the spiritual interests of their countrymen whom penury or oppression had driven to the Western Wilderness.

Among those who were led to devote themselves to ministerial labor on this side of the Atlantic was

Samuel Black, who was born in the Highlands of Scotland, and educated at Edinburgh.

Mr. Black came to America in 1734 or '35, with credentials, it is said, from the Synod of Glasgow, and was received, as a probationer, by the Presbytery of New Castle.

The Presbytery of Donegal, which was formed October 11, 1732, consisted at first of but four members.* This necessarily left a number of churches within its bounds without any stated ministry. In order to afford these destitute congregations an opportunity of hearing the preached word, the Presbytery of New Castle, in 1735–36, sent several of its probationers and others to supply the vacant pulpits. The Presbytery of Donegal resented this, and required all who occupied pulpits within its jurisdiction to be members of that body or, if probationers, that they should be examined and licensed by the Presbytery. Accordingly, when the congregation in this place applied for Mr. Black to preach for them as a candidate for "settlement," he obtained his dismissal from the Presbytery of New Castle, and placed himself under the care of the Presbytery of Donegal.

He was taken on "trials" May 23, 1736, preached before Presbytery on Romans viii. 31, lectured on the CXIX. Psalm, and read an Exegesis in Latin on De supremo judice contraversiam religionis.

At the next meeting of the Presbytery, October 27, 1736, after further examination and the delivery

---

* They were Anderson, of Donegal; Bertram, of Derry; Orr, of Lower Octoraro (Nottingham); and Boyd, of Upper Octoraro.

of discourses on Romans v. 1, and also on Romans viii. 8, he was licensed to preach the Gospel.

Mr. Black having accepted a second call from the Congregation in this place to become their pastor, the Presbytery, at the same meeting, appointed the second Wednesday in the November following for his ordination and installation.

According to this appointment, he was ordained and installed pastor of the Presbyterian Church in the Forks of Brandywine on the 10th of November, 1736. James Anderson, of Donegal, presided and preached from 1 Thess. v. 12 and 13. The only other ministers present were Alexander Craighead, of Middle Octoraro, and Ghelston, late the pastor of New London, who had recently joined the Presbytery of Donegal, and was then supplying Pequea and other places.

Mr. Black had been settled but a short time in the pastorate when the controversy which agitated and finally divided the Presbyterian Church caused dissensions among his people. Firmly attached to the doctrines and practices of the Old Side, he, perhaps, was not as reserved in expressing his opinions of the "Revivalists" as prudence dictated, nor as guarded in conduct as his position and the watchfulness of those who differed from him in their religious views demanded. These mistakes, however, would scarcely have led a majority of the members of his church to bring forward and earnestly press rancorous charges against him if the flames of discord had not been fanned by some of his ministerial brethren.

Foremost among these was David Anderson, who,

in October, 1739, had been installed pastor of the church in Pequea. Being a zealous partisan of the New Side, and believing it to be his duty, as he said, to carry the Gospel to a people burdened with a lifeless ministry, he intruded without hesitation within the bounds of Black's charge, and caused the estrangement of many of his flock from their pastor. Black appealed to the Presbytery for redress, but Anderson refused to obey a citation to appear before that body.

In consequence of these alienations and dissensions, twelve charges against Mr. Black were presented to the Presbytery at its meeting in September, 1740. The principal of these charges were drunkenness, sowing dissensions among his people, and a neglect of ministerial work. In the beginning of the November next following the Presbytery heard the charges, and rebuked, but did not suspend him.

As the manifest intention of the accusers of Mr. Black was to have his pulpit declared vacant, and the decision of the Presbytery did not accomplish that object, the charges, accompanied by the assertion that much important testimony had been kept back, were renewed at the meeting of Presbytery, in May, 1741. The Presbytery postponed the hearing until inquiries could be made on the spot, but, in deference to the importunities of his accusers, suspended him until the examination had taken place.

In the mean time the Synod, then the highest judicial tribunal of the Presbyterian Church, met in Philadelphia, the celebrated Protest, signed by Robert Cross and others, was read, June 1, 1741, the New

Brunswick brethren withdrew and formed a separate Synod, and the Presbyterian Church was "rent in twain."

In the following month the Presbytery met in this place, heard the testimony in support of the charges, and after a careful investigation, considered them unsustained, and restored Mr. Black. As a majority, however, of the congregation had attached themselves to the New Side, and those who remained were too few to support a stated ministry, the Presbytery dissolved the pastoral relation.

In October, 1738, the people of Conewago asked and obtained leave to be erected into a congregation. They also received permission to build a meeting-house in what is now the southern part of Dauphin County.* August 1, 1741, they presented a call to Mr. Black to become their pastor. This he accepted at the meeting of Presbytery in the October following (27th), and was installed on the second Wednesday of May, 1742.

In 1743 he spent part of his time laboring in Central Virginia, then the missionary field of both branches of the Presbyterian Church. For reasons which have not been stated, he applied for a dissolution of the pastoral relation in June, 1744, which the Presbytery refused.

March 26, 1745, he received a call from the congre-

---

* The congregation of Conewago remained but a comparatively short time as a distinct organization. The meeting-house, which stood near to where the turnpike road leading from Downingtown to Harrisburg crosses Conewago Creek, has long since disappeared. Traces of the graveyard belonging to it were visible in 1852.

gations of North and of South Mountain, Virginia, and again asked to be released from his charge at Conewago, assigning as reasons for removal the weakness and fewness of the people. The next April Presbytery granted his request and assigned him to North and South Mountain. But his people at Conewago, desirous of retaining him, made proposals which were satisfactory, and he remained with them. The Presbytery, at its meeting in September, ordered him to be reprimanded for not obeying his instructions, but complied with the request of the Congregation of Conewago and reinstated him as their pastor.

Owing to the loss of a part of the Minutes of the Presbytery of Donegal, it cannot be ascertained when Mr. Black left Conewago. He seems, however, while occasionally supplying vacancies in Virginia, to have remained until the death of Hindman, whom he succeeded in the pastorate of Rockfish and Mountain Plain, Virginia. This was probably in the latter part of 1746, or early in 1747. During his connection with Rockfish and Mountain Plain, he supplied several of the vacant congregations in North Carolina.

In 1756 the Presbytery of Hanover, New Side, appointed supplies for Rockfish, and directed them "not to interfere with Mr. Black and his labors." These orders availed but little, for at a meeting, in July, 1759, of the lately reconstructed Presbytery of Hanover, with which he was then connected, "Some charges were brought against him by portions of his congregations as reasons why the Presbytery should send them another pastor." The Presbytery proceeded with great tenderness and caution, and the difficulties were in part adjusted, when he resigned. After this, although occasionally occupying the pulpit, he appears to have remained without any stated charge until his death, which occurred August 9, 1770.

In justice to Mr. Black, it should be borne in mind that although his conduct on some occasions was blameworthy, yet his ministry was embraced in a period of extreme agitation, when the bitterness of controversy divided not only every congregation of which he was the pastor, but also every congregation connected with the Presbytery of Donegal, and even the whole Presbyterian Church. A period when accusations were preferred and placed on record which in "peaceful times" would never have been made.

Dr. Foote, in his "Notices of Virginia," states that Mr. Black "was Orthodox in doctrine, and correct in his views of religious action and Christian principles, as was proved by the fact that a goodly number of pious people were found at Rockfish, and his successors in the pastorate there saw evidence that God had blessed the ministry of His word by him."

In 1740 he was directed to supply the church at Norriton once a quarter until the next meeting of Synod;* and in 1744 was appointed one of the

---

* Norriton, the oldest Presbyterian Church edifice in Montgomery County, and now in ruins, was built about 1720. Like many of the Churches of that denomination, it was injured during the Revolutionary war, and money was raised to repair it by a lottery. It was probably placed on land which had been previously set aside and used as a

Trustees of the school established by the Synod at New London, Chester County.* He was reappointed in 1745 and 1746, and in the latter year was placed on the committee chosen to answer the letter of President Clapp, of Yale College, respecting the admission of students to that institution. The next year he, Thompson, and Craige were directed by the Synod "to have the oversight of the vacancies in Virginia."

The remains of Mr. Black were interred on a farm which he purchased after his permanent settlement in Virginia, where his grave, with no other memorial than an unlettered stone, may still be seen. The farm, now in the possession of his only surviving grandson, Thomas Black, lies in Albemarle County, Va., a few miles from the eastern base of the Blue Ridge.

He left a family of four sons and two daughters. Some of them settled in Kentucky and other Western States. The youngest, Samuel, remained at the homestead. Many of his descendants still reside in that part of Virginia, and it is due to them to state that a majority of them adhere to the church of which their great-grandfather was a Pioneer Minister in Pennsylvania, Virginia, and North Carolina.†

---

graveyard. The Centennial Presbyterian Church, dedicated in 1876, was erected on ground belonging to the Norriton Church.

* See Appendix C.

† Minutes of the Synod of Philadelphia; of the Old Presbytery of Donegal; of the Presbytery of Hanover; Com. from Rev. Hugh Henry; Foote, "Sketches of Virginia, Second Series."

REV. ADAM BOYD.
Born 1692. Died 1768.

During the closing years of the Seventeenth Century and the first quarter of the Eighteenth, a number of emigrants from Scotland and the North of Ireland landed in New England. Owing, however, to the country being, to a considerable extent, pre-occupied by other denominations, and to some legal restrictions on religious freedom, the Irish and Scotch-Irish Presbyterians found a settlement there less congenial than they had anticipated. Many of their clergymen, as a consequence, became dissatisfied, and either returned to their native land, or chose the laborious duties of a pioneer minister, in comparatively unsettled colonies, where greater opportunities for the establishment of churches were afforded.

Among the latter was the Rev. Thomas Craighead, who came to New England in 1715, but, near the close of 1723, removed to Southeastern Pennsylvania, now the State of Delaware.

About seven years after Mr. Craighead's arrival in New England, Adam Boyd came as a probationer from the North of Ireland. Where Mr. Boyd was educated is not known, but as a majority of the Presbyterian clergymen, who first emigrated to America from Ireland and Scotland, were graduates of the University of Glasgow, he may have been an Alumnus of that venerable institution.

He supplied, for some time, the pulpit left vacant

at Dedham, Mass., by the death of the Rev. Joseph Belcher, and also officiated in other churches near Boston; but, having been disappointed in his expectation of a settlement, he concluded to return to his native country. An attachment, however, to a daughter of Mr. Craighead caused him to relinquish his design and seek a pastorate near to that gentleman in Pennsylvania.

In pursuance of this determination Mr. Boyd came to this State, and having presented credentials from Ireland, and commendatory letters* from Cotton Mather and other clergymen of New England to the Presbytery of New Castle, he was received as a licentiate by that body, July 29, 1724. At the same time he was sent as a supply to Octoraro, and directed to collect a congregation at Pequea. His labors at both places were so well received that at the meeting of the Presbytery in the September immediately following, Arthur Parke and Cornelius Rowan, Commissioners from Octoraro and Pequea, presented a call for him to become their pastor. This he accepted on the 6th of October, 1724, and as the representatives of the congregations urged his immediate installation, the Presbytery appointed Wednesday of the next week for that purpose.

In accordance with this arrangement the Presbytery met at Octoraro the 13th of October, 1724, and ordained and installed Mr. Boyd as pastor of the congregations of Octoraro and Pequea.

Craighead presided, and Hook, of Drawers, preached

---

* See Appendix D.

the ordination sermon. The other members of the Presbytery, present, were Gillespie, Thomas Evans, and Hutchinson.

The country being, at that time, sparsely settled, the ministry of Mr. Boyd extended over a large area. A score of Presbyterian Churches, and upwards of eighty belonging to other denominations are now organized in what were the bounds of his charge. He was truly a pioneer minister of the Gospel; in fact, the only stated pastor in all the territory now included in the Western part of Chester County, and what was then settled of the present county of Lancaster.*

In the large field thus intrusted to his care, his industry, zeal, and faithfulness produced abundant fruit. Donegal became able to sustain a pastor in 1727. Middle Octoraro was organized in the same year, and Fagg's Manor in 1730. Bertram was settled at Paxson and Derry, and Thompson at Chestnut Level, in 1732. Craighead was installed at Pequea in 1733, and the Forks of Brandywine obtained the services of Black in 1736.

But while the bounds of his charge were diminished by the organization of churches, and the settlement of pastors over congregations which he had been largely instrumental in gathering, his labors were interrupted by the division of the Presbyterian Church, which took place in 1741.

This Schism, which was caused chiefly by a differ-

---

* At that time there were no settlements "over the river," that is, West of the Susquehanna.

ence of views in regard to revivals and the qualification of candidates for the ministry, though ultimately overruled by the Great Head of the Church for good, retarded the progress of Presbyterianism in America. "Congregations were divided. Two churches were established in many places where there was not support for one. Clergymen personally esteeming one another were debarred from an exchange of pulpits,"* while energy and ability which should have been employed in the furtherance of the Gospel were wasted in needless debate and acrimonious controversy.

But, in time, both parties saw their mistake. The New Side, or those who had considered a liberal education of minor importance as a qualification for the ministry, acknowledged their error by founding the College of New Jersey, with the avowed purpose of preparing young men to become heralds of the Gospel. On the other hand, their opponents, the Old Side, were convinced by the increasing number and ability of those who were leaders of the "great awakening" in the churches that learning, unaccompanied by earnest, vital piety, is insufficient for the extension of the Redeemer's Kingdom. As a consequence, after seventeen years of separation, the breach was healed.

In the mean time, Mr. Boyd ministered to the members of his flock who had not wandered from the fold, and on the 11th of August, 1741, accepted an invitation to preach one-half of his time to those in this place who had been left without a pastor by the withdrawal of Mr. Black.

---

* Dr. Miller's Life of Rodgers.

As a majority of the congregation had seceded, the number that remained was not large; but after the death of Mr. Dean, and the failure of the New Side to obtain a settled pastor, the attendance on Mr. Boyd's ministrations increased. Indeed, it could hardly have been otherwise, since many of them had been brought to a knowledge of the Saviour by his preaching before the organization of a church in this part of his charge. During his connection with the congregation upwards of one hundred and twenty, many of them heads of families, contributed toward the payment of his salary, and they may not have been a majority of his hearers.*

In October, 1758, the pastoral relation was, as he has recorded, "dissolved in a most irregular manner." Why is not known. Perhaps some members of the church were displeased with his assent to the terms of the Union, and requested that another should be sent in his stead, or the Presbytery may have acted without being fully acquainted with the wishes of the larger portion of the congregation. But whatever may have been the cause of his irregular and abrupt dismissal, all will admit that it was undeserved. He surely was worthy of kind and respectful treatment who, during seventeen years, had travelled ten miles every other Sabbath and conducted religious services for the annual stipend of a little more than fifty dollars.

After the close of his pastorate at "the Forks," the members of the Old Side congregation at Octo-

---

* See Appendix E.

raro agreed to pay for two-thirds of his time, instead of one-half as they had previously done. This arrangement continued until April, 1768, when Mr. Boyd, "by reason of his feeble health, requested the Presbytery to send supplies for his pulpit as often as possible."

A few months afterward, the congregation united with the New Side in a call to the Rev. William Forster to take charge of both congregations. This call, which Mr. Boyd heartily approved, Mr. Forster accepted, and on the 19th of October, 1768, was installed pastor of the "United Congregation of Upper Octoraro." On account of his long connection with the congregation and his faithful services, the pastoral relation of Mr. Boyd was not dissolved, and his people agreed to pay him twenty-five pounds yearly during the remainder of his life. But the "time of his departure was at hand." He died on the 19th of November, 1768, in the forty-sixth year of his ministry.

His remains were interred in the adjoining graveyard, and the record on his tombstone states that he was "eminent through life for modest piety, diligence in his office, prudence, equanimity, and peace."

He left a widow, five sons, and five daughters. His widow survived him nearly eleven years, or until November 9, 1779. His eldest son, John, studied for the ministry, but died shortly after his licensure.

Thomas was settled by his father on an adjoining farm. He died in 1778. The property is still in the possession of his descendants.

Andrew inherited the homestead. He was an ardent patriot during the Revolutionary War, attained the rank of colonel, and acted as commissary for Chester County nearly the whole of that trying period.

Adam became a resident of North Carolina, was editor of the *Cape Fear Mercury* in 1767, a leading member of the Committee of Safety of that State, and, in 1776, chaplain of a North Carolina Brigade.

Samuel pursued his preparatory studies at McDowell's School, Maryland; entered the Medical Department of the University of Pennsylvania in 1764, and settled as a physician in Virginia.

Three of the daughters were married to clergymen: Janet to the Rev. Robert McMordie, then pastor of Marsh Creek and Round Hill, in Lancaster, now York, County; Agnes to the Rev. Sampson Smith, pastor at Chestnut Level; and Margaret to the Rev. Joseph Tate, at that time pastor of Donegal.

The Rev. Matthew Tate, son of the last mentioned, was licensed by the Presbytery of New Castle, and employed as a supply by that and other Presbyteries. He subsequently entered the Episcopal Church, and some years previous to his death, in October, 1795, was rector of a parish in South Carolina.

The Rev. Andrew B. Cross, an able and popular clergyman of Baltimore, Mrs. Webster, widow of the lamented historian of the Presbyterian Church, and many of the most influential and respectable citizens of Sadsbury, and the adjoining Townships of Chester County, are descendants of Adam Boyd.

In the management of his worldly affairs, Mr. Boyd was economical, exact, and careful. Although his salary never exceeded three hundred dollars a year, and was frequently less, and a part of that was paid in produce and some in labor, yet he acquired considerable property. His daughters received marriage portions, which were regarded as large "in those days." Three of his sons were educated for the learned professions, and his other sons were comfortably settled on farms which their father had purchased.

Like pioneer ministers in general, Mr. Boyd was too much occupied with the discharge of his pastoral duties to prepare any of his discourses for the press. Some of his sermons have been preserved, but they are written in a kind of short-hand, which is difficult to decipher. We are, therefore, without the means of knowing either the arrangement, style, or tenor of his pulpit exercises; but his discretion, piety, and faithfulness lead to the conclusion that his remarks in the pulpit were well calculated to confirm the faith, arouse the conscience, and enliven the hopes of those whom he addressed. Following the example of the Apostle to the Gentiles, he, no doubt, "reasoned of temperance, righteousness, and judgment to come." But his hearers, unlike the profligate viceroy of the Roman Emperor, were not ignorant of that blessed Gospel for whose sake many of them had abandoned the land of their birth and made the wilderness their home.*

---

* Futhey, "Hist. of Upper Octoraro Church;" Webster, "Hist. of Presb. Church;" Minutes of Donegal Presbytery; Com. from Rev. Andrew B. Cross.

REV. WILLIAM DEAN.
Born 1719. Died 1748.

The exciting controversies, self-denying labor, and severe trials of the Presbyterian Churches in Scotland and Ireland during the Sixteenth and Seventeenth Centuries were succeeded towards the close of the latter by listlessness and a lack of earnestness. Warm appeals to the impenitent, and the zeal for the extension of the Redeemer's kingdom, which characterized the earlier history of the church, gave place to doctrinal explanations and long sermons delivered in a cold and didactic manner. Learning and orthodoxy were more regarded in the selection of pastors than vital piety. As a consequence a laxity of morals prevailed. Intemperance became common, and profanity was often heard from those who were the professed followers of the Divine author of the command, "Swear not at all."

This indifference to spiritual interests continued until the close of the first quarter of the Eighteenth Century, when both pastors and people were aroused from their lethargy by the faithful labors of the Wesleys and Whitefield in the British Islands, and of Whitefield and the Tennents in America. The Log College, established by the last mentioned, sent forth a number of young men, whose warmth, earnestness, and energy were in strong contrast with learned but frigid discourses which failed to arouse the conscience or amend the heart. Their hearers retired not to discuss the bearing and correctness of creeds or the errors of Romanism, but anxiously inquiring, "What must we do to be saved?"

Among those who were deeply imbued with the spirit and zeal of Whitefield and the graduates of the Log College was William Dean, who came from the North of Ireland to America in 1739 or '40. Where he was educated is not known. He probably received his academical training in his native country, and his theological under the direction of the Tennents.

He was taken on trials by the Presbytery of New Brunswick, August 3, 1741, and assigned the following subjects "to found discourses upon." For an English sermon, Rom. iii. 19; and for an Exegesis, *An homo justificatur ab eterno an tempore?*

At a meeting of the Presbytery, held at Freehold, N. J., in October, 1742, he and Charles Beatty having passed satisfactory trials and examinations, were licensed (October 13) "to preach the everlasting Gospel where Providence may direct them."

Mr. Dean was sent by the Presbytery, immediately after his licensure, to Neshaminy, Bucks County, and the settlements on the Forks of Delaware. These were made, in 1730 or '32, by Presbyterians from the North of Ireland. The one on the West Fork, the Lehigh, being called Craig's settlement, and the one on the North Fork, the Delaware, Hunter's settlement.

The country was mostly a wilderness, inhabited by the Lenni Lenape, or Delaware Indians. Efforts were made by the devoted Brainerd and others to bring them to a knowledge of the saving truths of the Gospel, though with little apparent success. They were strongly attached to their favorite places of abode and hunting-grounds, and did not abandon them until they were forced to remove by the "Five Nations."

In 1743, Dean was appointed to supply Craig's and Hunter's settlements and Cape May, and in the Fall of the same year he was sent by the New Side Presbytery of New Castle, with which he was then connected, to Pequea and the "Forks of Brandywine."

In 1744 he was directed to preach at Cohansey, now Fairfield, N. J., and the Forks of Delaware, and in the following year he went, with Byram, of Mendham, N. J., to Augusta County, Va., where their labors were followed by a great revival.

In 1745 he received and accepted a second call from the New Side Congregation in this place to become their pastor, and was installed in May or June of that year. But his labor in a field which seemed likely to produce an abundant harvest was soon ended. In a little more than three years his flock was left without a shepherd, and the New Side Presbytery of New Castle had sustained the loss of one of its youngest and most promising members.

The invitations which Mr. Dean received to remain in the settlements to which he was sent as an occasional or a stated supply; the revival which followed his missionary efforts in Virginia, and the regret expressed on account of his early death by some of the ablest of his contemporaries, confirm the uniform tradition that he was a popular, zealous, and faithful minister of the Gospel.

In 1743 three calls for his services were presented to Presbytery,—one from the Forks of Delaware, another from the Forks of Brandywine, and a third from

Cape May. These he held under consideration for a time and declined. In May, 1748, a few weeks before his death, a similar request* was sent to the Synod of New Brunswick from Timber Bridge and the Forks of James River, Virginia.

The Rev. Samuel Davies, afterwards President of the College of New Jersey, writing from Virginia to Dr. Bellamy, of Bethlehem, Connecticut, in 1751, speaks of the death of Mr. Dean in the same affectionate terms in which he records the loss of those "eminent men of God," William Robinson and Samuel Blair. He also states that the blessed effects of the revival which had followed the labors of Byram and Dean were still manifest.

During his connection with the congregation in this place, Mr. Dean resided in a house which stood a short distance east of the dwelling of Mr. Francis Growe, in West Nantmeal Township. That house, which, like all in the neighborhood, was built of unhewn logs, the members of his church caused to be wainscoted and weather-boarded, thus making it superior, both in comfort and appearance, to the rude and unplastered structures which constituted their own places of abode.

The remains of Dean were interred in the "lower graveyard," where his tomb, which bears the following inscription, may be seen:

> "Here lieth the Body of
> The Reverend William Dean
> Who departed this Life
> July 9th 1748.
> Aged 29 Years.

* See Appendix F.

In yonder sacred House I spent my Breath
Now silent, mouldering, here I ly in Death
These silent Lips shall wake and yet declare
A dread Amen to truths they published there."

It is, perhaps, worthy of remark, that this inscription, with the omission of the word *silent* in the line preceding the last and the necessary change of name, date, and age, is the same as the record on the tomb of the Rev. Samuel Blair in the burial-ground at Fagg's Manor, also on the gravestone of the Rev. John Campbell in the church-yard at Providence, Montgomery County, and with a slight change on the tombstone of the Rev. Owen Thomas in Vincent burial-ground. It was probably written by the Rev. Samuel Davies.

Although all that was mortal of Dean has mingled with the earth in this " Country Church-Yard," far from kindred and his native land, yet He who never slumbers watches his dust, and the Church cherishes a grateful remembrance of one who was so quickly spent " laboring to save and to bless."

Dean left a widow, four sons, Joseph, Benjamin, who died when near his majority, William, John, and a daughter, Sarah. After the death of her husband Mrs. Dean resided some years on the farm which they had patented, but probably on account of the education of her children removed to Philadelphia.* There, Joseph became a successful importing merchant and a noted actor in the stirring events of the latter half of the Eighteenth Century. He was one of the signers of the

---

* Her name is on the list of taxables in West Nantmeal Township for 1753.

Non-Importation Resolutions adopted October (25th) 1765, and at the beginning of the Revolutionary War loaned the General Government sixty thousand dollars, which were never returned.

He was selected by the Assembly in December, 1776, to serve on the Committee of Safety, and was an active member of the Board of War from its organization, in March, 1777, until it was discontinued, in August of the same year.

In January, 1781, Joseph Dean was appointed one of the auditors to settle and adjust the accounts of the troops of the State of Pennsylvania in the service of the United States, and in the Autumn of the same year a Warden of the Port of Philadelphia.

John held the rank of Major in the Continental Army, and William as Colonel in the same service was actively engaged in all the battles which were fought in New Jersey.

Sarah was married to the Rev. John Slemmons, a native of Chester County and a graduate of the College of New Jersey, who, in 1765, became pastor of Lower Marsh Creek Church in York, now Adams, County, Pennsylvania. Mr. Slemmons was subsequently pastor of Piney Creek Church, Maryland, where he remained until his death, in 1814. Mrs. Slemmons died in June, 1823, and her ashes rest beside those of her husband in the Piney Creek graveyard.

A grandson of Colonel William Dean, William F. Dean, Esq., a gentleman of wealth and influence, has long resided in Philadelphia.*

---

* Minutes of Synod of New Brunswick; Archives of State, vol. i. p. 9; Memoranda of Springton Manor; Hist. of Piney Creek Church.

REV. JOHN CARMICHAEL.

Born 1728. Died 1785.

Civil war had ceased in England and a stable government had been established in that portion of Great Britain more than half a century before discord and violence were repressed in Scotland. The attachment of many of the nobles to the "House of Stuart," the hereditary feuds of the clans, and the inroads of heartless marauders were a continual source of disorder and bloodshed. The oppression and suffering which the inhabitants as a consequence endured led many of them to emigrate to countries where law and order were supreme, and where man could enjoy the fruits of his labor without annoyance from petty chiefs or the followers of royal pretenders.

Among those whom the "troublesome times" caused to leave their native land were David and Elizabeth (Alexander) Carmichael, who came from Argyleshire to America in 1737. They settled first at Hackensack, New Jersey, but after a short residence there removed to Newark in the same State.

Having been exemplary members of the established church in Scotland, Mr. Carmichael and his wife connected themselves with the Presbyterian Church in Newark, then or shortly afterwards under the pastoral charge of the Rev. Aaron Burr. The preaching of this able divine, and especially his earnest appeals to the unconverted at the administration of the Lord's Supper, made a deep impression on the mind of their eldest son, and induced a serious consideration of his condition as a sinner. The counsels of Christian friends, aided by the prayers and example of his pious mother, led him as an humble penitent to the Throne of Mercy, where he obtained pardon and peace. Anxious that others should be brought to a knowledge of the Saviour and share in the comfort and reconciliation which he had found, he determined to devote himself to the Christian ministry. He became a member of the College of New Jersey in 1755, and received the degree of A.B. in August, 1759. Where he pursued his studies previous to entering the College is not known. But as the institution was then located at Newark, he probably received his preparatory training under the direction of his pastor, the Rev. Aaron Burr, President of the College.

Nine of the eighteen members of his class entered the Gospel ministry. All of them living at the time proved faithful to their country in its hour of trial, and the suffering patriotic efforts and tragic death of one of them, the lamented Caldwell, of Elizabethtown, have become matters of history.

"Immediately after he was graduated Mr. Carmichael commenced the study of theology under the direction of the President of the College, the Rev. Samuel Davies."

He pursued his theological studies with so much diligence and success that at a meeting of the Presbytery of New Brunswick, held in May, 1760, he was licensed to preach the Gospel.

Mr. Carmichael spent the remainder of that year in supplying vacancies by the direction of the Synod.

Among them was the unoccupied pulpit of this church. His preaching here was so acceptable that on the 18th of September, 1760, the members of session addressed him a letter entreating him to become their pastor.* This he seems, while continuing to occupy the pulpit, to have held for consideration. The congregation, however, determined, if possible, to obtain his services, and on the 13th of April, 1761, presented a call to Presbytery, which was referred to him. Having sought Divine Guidance by fasting and prayer, he accepted it, and on Thursday, the 23d of April, 1761, was ordained and installed pastor of the Church of the Forks of Brandywine by the Presbytery of New Castle.

At that period the country was sparsely settled and the inhabitants for the most part in moderate circumstances. One of the meeting-houses was no longer in a condition to be used as a place for public worship, and the other, though in a better state of repair, was too small to accommodate all who assembled on the Sabbath. The efforts, therefore, of Mr. Carmichael, immediately after his installation, were directed to obtain the erection of a building suitable for the services of the sanctuary. Infusing his own zeal into every one with whom he came in contact, he succeeded, during the first year of his pastorate, in having the large and commodious meeting-house built which has recently been taken down.

In the pulpit his manner was earnest and impressive. While he dwelt with frequency and power on the terrors of the law, he also faithfully reminded those who

---
* See Appendix G.

were weighed down by the burden of sin, "that there was balm in Gilead, and a Physician there."

Although strongly attached to the creed and form of church government in his fatherland, he considered them of small importance in comparison with Godliness and an interest in the Atoning Sacrifice. His labors among the people of his charge were greatly blessed. Harmony was restored, the wanderers returned to the fold, and not a few who had been cavilling about points of doctrine were led to make the all-important inquiry, "How shall we be made partakers of the blessings of the Covenant of Grace?"

He visited the members of his congregation not only *statedly* but *frequently*. On these occasions the household was called together for prayer, and the younger members of the family recited the Shorter Catechism, and happy were the little ones who could "say their questions" in a manner which received the approving smile and kind words of Mr. Carmichael.

As many of his people resided at a distance of seven or eight miles from the place for public worship, and buildings for school purposes were few, he frequently preached at private houses on the afternoon of the Sabbath. He also made missionary journeys into parts of this and some of the adjoining States where no church was organized, besides frequently assisting his ministerial brethren at the administration of the ordinances, and by occupying their pulpits when sickness or other circumstances caused them to be absent from their charge. But these were not his only labors.

The detail of kingly and ecclesiastical tyranny which Mr. Carmichael had often heard from parental lips made him the determined foe of oppression in every form. Before the Revolutionary Conflict he observed the cloud of war which loomed in the horizon, and by a series of articles in the public papers warned his fellow-citizens of their danger. And when the storm did come, he was among the foremost to breast its fury and provide means to repair the devastation which it caused. In the pulpit and at the fireside, among the members of his flock and where he was known only by name, he was equally bold in the denunciation of tyranny and faithful in portraying the blessings of freedom.

When the First Congress[*] met in Philadelphia he called on the members personally urging them to action, and after they adjourned he admonished those who remained and others from the pulpit, as is shown by the following extract from the journal of John Adams:

"Sunday, March 26th, 1775, went to hear Mr. Carmichael preach at Mr. Duffield's church on Trust in the Lord, and do good; so shalt thou dwell in the land, and verily thou shalt be fed."[†]

In June, 1775, he preached a sermon from Luke iii. 14, to the militia of Lancaster, in which he strongly advocated the lawfulness of self-defence. This sermon was published, had a wide-spread salutary effect, and soon passed to a second edition.[‡]

---

[*] The First Congress, composed of delegates from all the Colonies except Georgia, met in Philadelphia, September 5, 1774. It consisted of fifty-two members, and was in session fifty-two days.

[†] Psalm xxxvii. 3.

[‡] It is the only production of his pen, except some articles in the newspapers, that was ever printed.

Mr. Carmichael delivered a spirited address shortly before their departure to the Volunteers from the upper part of Chester County, who left their homes on the 8th of July, 1776, to join the army near New York. As many of them were members of his church, and a number of them had been led to volunteer by his appeals to their love of country, he seems to have visited them not long after they had reached their destination, for he and the Rev. Robert Smith, of Pequea, were present at the battle of Long Island, which took place on the 27th of the next August.

But if his ardor, activity, and influence were so fully required immediately after the Declaration of Independence, they were still more needed in the following year, when his adopted State became the theatre of warlike operations.

The cannonading at the battle of Brandywine was distinctly heard throughout all this section of the country. During the progress of that engagement wives, daughters, and mothers stood at the doors of their dwellings listening with fearful anxiety, and as the report of each discharge of artillery fell on the ear, were rendered almost frantic by the thought that it had caused the death of a husband, a father, or a son.

The disastrous result of that battle, the appearance of parties of British horsemen in search of forage, and the conveyance of a large number of wounded American soldiers along the Paxtang Road to Ephrata for medical treatment, caused general consternation and terror.* Some whose fears were greater than their

* Upwards of One Hundred and Fifty of them died and were buried at Ephrata.

patriotism passed over to the enemy; others sought safety by flight; while the loyal few that had remained at home, who were capable of performing military duty, hastened to join their brethren in the field. During this trying period, when there was a vacant chair at almost every fireside, the labor and the trials of the faithful pastor and ardent patriot were unceasing. At one time consoling those whose relatives had fallen in the conflict, at another reviving the hopes and dispelling the fears of many who were ready to exclaim, "All is lost." On week-days assisting aged men, women, and children in the out-door employments of the farm; on the Sabbath fervently beseeching the Supreme Disposer of events to end the evils of war by the final triumph of the cause of Liberty and of Humanity.

Mr. Carmichael visited the American army when it lay at Valley Forge, and having learned from General Washington that the wounded were suffering from a want of linen for bandages, he returned home, called his congregation together, stated the fact, and earnestly besought the female members of his charge to furnish a supply, even if it should require an abbreviation of portions of their clothing. The appeal was successful. A sufficient number of packages of linen were obtained to fill two bags. These he conveyed on horseback to the camp.

A letter is extant in which the Commander-in-chief thanks Mr. Carmichael and his congregation for the supply of clothing and other necessaries which they had furnished for the use of the army.

The war was finally brought to a close, the independence of our country was acknowledged, and Mr.

Carmichael thankfully devoted himself to a discharge of the duties of his Sacred Office. But his physical system, never strong, had been weakened by his unceasing exertions in the cause of religion and of civil liberty. His health declined, and he became aware that the time of his departure was near. He arranged his temporal affairs,* and with increased zeal in his Master's service, preached a course of sermons on Haggai i. 10. "The design of these discourses was to show that there are times when the servants of God should more than ordinarily engage in the promotion of religion."

In the latter part of October, 1785, he assisted the Rev. Dr. Smith, of Pequea, in the communion of that church. His efforts during the service, and the fatigue of the journey, brought on an illness from which he had not recovered when the administration of the ordinances to his own people took place. On that occasion his bodily weakness, increased by the exertion which he had then made, led him to express the opinion "that he would no more drink wine with them until he drank it new in his Father's Kingdom." An opinion whose correctness was too soon verified. Exposure to the rain on his return home, together with his previous debility, induced an attack of pleurisy, which caused his death on the 15th of November, 1785, when he had entered less than three weeks on his fifty-eighth year.†

His last words were, "Oh that I had a thousand

---

* See Appendix II.
† He was born on the 28th of October, 1728.

tongues, that I might employ them all in bringing sinners to Christ!"

His remains lie in the Upper Graveyard beside the ashes of his eldest daughter, and those of the two partners of his joys and sorrows, "who preceded him to the eternal world."

The labors of Mr. Carmichael as a patriot and a pastor, his energy, faithfulness, and success, lead to the belief that, like holy men of old, he was raised up and specially prepared for the work which God had appointed for him to do. He seems to have combined, in a remarkable degree, the glowing zeal and vital piety of Whitefield and the Tennents, with the bold advocacy of civil and religious liberty which distinguished Scotland's great reformer, "the fearless Knox."

Mr. Carmichael was married in May, 1761, to Miss Phœbe Cram, of Newark, New Jersey, a granddaughter of the Rev. Jonathan Dickinson, first President of the College of New Jersey. She died October 21, 1772, in her forty-second year, leaving a son and a daughter. Two other children having died in infancy.

The son, John Flavel, studied medicine under Dr. Scott, of New Brunswick, New Jersey, practised for some time in this neighborhood with success, entered the army as a surgeon in 1788, and after holding the office several years settled in the State of Mississippi, where he accumulated considerable property, and died in 1837.

The daughter, Phœbe, for nearly sixty years an humble and upright member of the Presbyterian

Church at Cedar Grove, Lancaster County, died March 24, 1859, at the advanced age of ninety-two years and nearly two months.

In June, 1773, Mr. Carmichael married Miss Catharine Mustard. But this union was of short duration. She died in August, 1774, leaving a daughter fifteen days old, who received the name of her mother. That daughter, on the death of her father, was taken in charge and kindly cared for by Elder William Hunter, a leading member of the congregation. She subsequently resided with the Rev. Dr. Smith, of Pequea, and also in the family of Mr. Buckley until her marriage, in September, 1799, to the Hon. Robert Jenkins, a gentleman of wealth and refinement.

Mrs. Jenkins closed a life noted for kindness to the poor, a liberal support of churches and benevolent associations, and a consistent Christian course, on the 23d of September, 1856, in the eighty-third year of her age. Both of her sons had preceded their mother to the grave. Four of her daughters were married to ministers of the Gospel eminent for learning and ability.

By his marriage, in April, 1775, to a daughter of the Rev. Samuel Blair, of Fagg's Manor, Mr. Carmichael had three children. Elizabeth, who became the wife of the Rev. Samuel Donnell, subsequently a pastor in the Cumberland Presbyterian Church. They removed to Tennessee, where her death occurred shortly after their arrival. Washington Gates, born about the time of Burgoyne's surrender, and named in honor of the commander-in-chief and the hero of Saratoga, entered the army, but died soon afterwards near the mouth of the Mississippi. Francina, the youngest, was married to a Captain Allan.

Mrs. Carmichael survived her husband nearly a quarter of a century, or until May, 1810; and Mrs. Allan died in the latter part of December, 1870.*

---

* Sprague, "Annals of American Pulpit;" Minutes of Presbytery of Newcastle; of Synod of New Brunswick; Dr. Leaman, "Memorial of Mrs. C. M. Jenkins;" Local Memoranda; Dr. S. Alexander, "Princeton College in the Eighteenth Century."

REV. NATHAN GRIER.

Born 1760. Died 1814.

Biography often affords manifest and instructive proofs that the Author of All Good watches over, guides, and blesses not only those who serve Him and keep His commandments, but also their children to the third, fourth, and succeeding generations.

Among American statesmen there has been no one who was more upright in public and in private life than John Adams, and of him only can it be stated that the Presidential Chair, in which he was placed as the immediate successor of Washington, was also occupied by his son. Nor is this all. His son and grandson discharged with ability the duties of Minister Plenipotentiary to England, where he had appeared as his country's first Ambassador.

As might be expected, however, the lives of those who specially devote themselves to the service of the altar present numerous instances of the Providence of God in blessing their descendants, and not unfrequently in making them "shepherds and bishops of souls."[*]

A number of pulpits, both in the Presbyterian Church and those of other denominations, are occu-

---

[*] Dr. Spring stated in 1849, that not less than seventy ministers in the American Church could trace their lineage to the elder Edwards, who was himself the son of a clergyman.

pied at the present time by the sons and grandsons of men who passed their lives in the same sacred calling.

A notable example, however, of pious ancestors, and of children who trod in the footsteps of their fathers, is afforded by the parentage and descendants of the Rev. Nathan Grier.

John and Matthew Grier came to America from the North of Ireland in 1732. Shortly after his arrival John married Agnes Caldwell, and settled in Bucks County, Pa. Like their Scotch ancestors, they were strongly attached to the doctrines and institutions of the Presbyterian Church, of which they were for many years exemplary members. Their children were trained "in the nurture and admonition of the Lord," and as a reward for their faithful oversight they had the satisfaction of seeing two of them enter the ministry, and all of them become worthy and useful members of society.

Nathan, the younger of those who entered the ministry, was born in September, 1760. Naturally amiable and contemplative, while still quite young his thoughts were turned to the subject of religion, and, like Josiah, he early gave his heart to God.

Having resolved to devote himself to the preaching of the Gospel, he passed through his preparatory training under the direction of his brother James,[*] who was also his theological preceptor, entered the University of Pennsylvania in 1781, and was graduated in 1783. After leaving the University, he taught a school at Pitt's Grove, N. J., pursuing at the same time his studies in theology.

[*] See Appendix M.

Mr. Grier was licensed by the Presbytery of Philadelphia in October, 1786, and passed the remainder of that year and a part of the next in supplying churches without a pastor. Among them was the congregation worshipping in this place. His labors here led to a unanimous call from the members of the church to become their pastor being placed in his hands and accepted.

On Wednesday, the 22d of August, 1787, the Presbytery of New Castle, with which he was then connected, met here, and ordained and installed him pastor of the Presbyterian Church of the Forks of Brandywine. The Rev. Alexander Mitchell, pastor of Doe Run Church, preached the sermon; the other ministers present were Robert Smith, D.D., James Anderson, William R. Smith, Nathaniel W. Sample, John E. Finley, John McCreery, James Monroe, David Jones, and John Burton.

Mr. Grier, at that time in the full vigor of his powers, was well adapted to carry on the work which Mr. Carmichael had so auspiciously begun. Earnest, impressive, and practical, his ministrations were greatly blessed. The attendance on the Sabbath rapidly increased, and his influence, aided by his popular manners, soon reached far beyond even the large area contained within the bounds of his charge.

Having early perceived that the services of the sanctuary are but a part of the duties of a pastor, he frequently called at the residences of the members of his congregation. These visits were not permitted to pass unimproved, but were used as opportunities for pious instruction. Parents were mildly but faithfully reminded of the obligations resting upon them; the children were questioned in regard to their acquaintance with the Catechism and their knowledge of religious principles; and the whole household humbly and reverently bowed in prayer, while their pastor earnestly invoked the Divine Blessing on the heads of the family and their offspring.

Instructed by the glimpse of the Eternal World afforded by the parable of Dives and Lazarus, he avoided the mistake which clergymen often make, of frequent visits to the mansions of the wealthy while the dwellings of those of stinted means are passed unnoticed. Such, too, was his amiability and warmth of feeling that he was equally welcomed at the homes of the poorest and the richest members of his congregation.

In addition to the weekly ministrations of the pulpit, he preached during the Summer, on the afternoon of the Sabbath, either in school-houses or at the residences of the aged and infirm. He also assisted his clerical brethren at Communion seasons and on other occasions, and frequently supplied the pulpit of congregations without a pastor. Among the latter was the church at Upper Octoraro, during the fourteen years it was without a regular ministry, before the installation of the Rev. James Latta. On these occasions the house was crowded, the attention close, and the impressions made deep and often lasting.

As his predecessor, Mr. Carmichael, adding the duties of the patriot to those of the pastor, labored with assiduity to aid the cause of civil liberty and enlist soldiers to combat the enemies of national independence, Mr. Grier, combining the pastor and the theological instructor, and working with equal zeal and watchfulness, prepared young men to engage in a holier war under the Great Captain of Salvation.

It is well known that a hundred years were permitted to pass, after the establishment of the Presbyterian Church in America, before a Seminary was organized and endowed by the Church for the special study of theology. Candidates for the ministry were, therefore, trained by eminent divines in schools opened for that purpose. The Log College, Blair's School at Fagg's Manor, Allison's School at New London, and Smith's School in Pequea, were established mainly with this object in view.

Mr. Grier, a well-read theologian, following their example, received a number of young men, and especially those of his own congregation, under his care, for the study of Theology.

This Divinity School, though not formally known by that name, took the place of Dr. Smith's School in Pequea. It was commenced in 1792, when the infirmities of Dr. Smith, who died in April, 1793, rendered him incapable of directing the studies of young men preparing to enter the ministry.

The following synopsis of the course pursued by the students under the supervision of Mr. Grier is from the pen of the most eminent of his pupils, the Rev. Dr. McConaughy:

"Those who studied under his direction were accustomed to divide their time between the study of the Scriptures, Ecclesiastical History, and a series of questions about One Hundred in number, in the usual order of the System of Theology. On these questions they were required to write pretty fully and submit the result to his examination and criticism. In like manner they composed sermons, on which they had his opinion as to matter and style.

"Besides this, they had the advantages of his Christian example, the genial influence of his well-ordered household, and his daily counsel and guidance."

Of the twenty young men who studied Theology under the direction of Mr. Grier, one, Mr. John Ralston, died (in 1804) before the completion of his studies, and ill-health prevented another, Mr. John M'Clure, from entering on the active duties of the ministry. The remaining eighteen, as may be learned by the biographical sketches appended, became workers in the Gospel field. Seventeen of them were pastors of churches, and one passed upwards of thirty years as a Chaplain in the Navy of the United States.

Three received the honorary title of D.D., and one of both D.D. and LL.D., at a period when collegiate honors were not so freely dispensed as they are at present.

They occupied pulpits in six States of the Union, and all, with one exception, faithfully discharged the duties of their sacred office until they were unfitted by the infirmities of age or removed by death.

But his fellow-laborers in the Master's vineyard were suddenly deprived of an associate and the congregation of its pastor. He died, after a short illness, on the 30th of March, 1814, at the comparatively early age of fifty-three years and six months.

The inscription on his tombstone, in the Upper Graveyard, closes with the following terse and beautiful lines of Goldsmith, which have seldom been so correctly applied:

> "But in his duty prompt at every call,
> He watched and wept, he prayed and felt for all.
> He tried each art, reproved each dull delay,
> Allured to brighter worlds, and led the way."

Mr. Grier was punctual in his attendance on the councils of the church, in which he took an active, though not a forward, part. A leading trustee of Dickinson College during the latter years of his life, he watched over its interests with paternal solicitude, warmly advocated the establishing of a Theological Seminary, and ably sustained all the religious enterprises of his day.

Although his sermons, prepared with care, were evangelical and well illustrated by references to the Scriptures, they were practical rather than doctrinal or controversial. Gifted with a voice of more than ordinary power, Mr. Grier could be heard by a large audience, and he seldom failed to enchain the attention of his hearers by his earnestness, warmth, and direct appeals to the conscience. Indeed, if he displayed greater power in the pulpit in one direction more than another, it was in his ability to call forth the finer feelings of our nature, and arouse the dormant sympathies of the heart. He, therefore, often made salutary impressions which the lapse of years failed to erase. As an instance of this, the writer may state that he has heard the aged relate, while tears gathered in their eyes as the solemn scene came in remembrance before them, his touching appeals at the close of each Communion to the members of his church to live consistently with their profession, and the melting tenderness with which he besought those who " were strangers to the Covenant of Grace" to flee from the wrath to come.

Mr. Grier was united in marriage, November 13, 1787, to Miss Susannah Smith, daughter of Colonel Robert and Margaret Smith, members of his congregation. She was eminently worthy of his choice, and by her piety, prudence, and careful family oversight strengthened his hands and lessened his worldly cares. " But he was not permitted to enjoy her counsel and aid to the close of his life." On January 2, 1812, she exchanged the probation of time for the blessedness of eternity.

Their children were two sons and three daughters. Both of their sons entered the ministry, and stood as faithful sentinels for more than half a century on the watch-towers of Zion. Their eldest daughter was married to Mr. White, a quarter of a century the popular pastor of the church in Fagg's Manor. Another became the wife of Mr. Parke, who ministered with acceptance upwards of thirty years to the churches of Slate Ridge and Centre, in York County, Pa.; and the third, the much-esteemed widow of Dr. Thompson, of Fagg's Manor, was for several years previous to her decease a member of this congregation.

Six of the grandsons of Mr. Grier became ministers of the Gospel, and five of them are still engaged in proclaiming the glad tidings of Salvation. Those who survive are the eldest son of Mr. White, two of the sons of Mr. Robert S. Grier, one of the sons of Mr. Parke, and the younger son of Dr. Thompson. Another grandson, Dr. Nathan G. Thompson, is now a Ruling Elder in this congregation, where his grandfather and uncle declared the whole counsel of God upwards of fourscore years.

A discourse entitled "The Man of Bethany," commemorative of Mr. Grier, was delivered shortly after his death by the Rev. William Arthur, at that time pastor of the Pequea Presbyterian Church.*

---

* Sprague, " Annals of Pres. Church ;" Rev. J. N. C. Grier, D.D., " Historical Discourse ;" MS. Collections ; Minutes of the Presbytery of Newcastle.

REV. JOHN N. C. GRIER, D.D.

Born 1792. Died 1880.

In the Presbyterian Churches of Ireland and Scotland the settlement of a pastor in charge of a congregation is generally a settlement for life. The shepherd and his flock are seldom separated except by death. The hearers of "the man of God," venerable for years and piety, are frequently the grandchildren of those who welcomed him as their youthful pastor.

This unbroken, harmonious, and Christian relation between the people and their spiritual adviser, from his entrance on his ministry until its close, has not been confined to the Eastern shore of the Atlantic. Instances of the pastor "who ne'er had changed or wished to change his place" are not uncommon in the history of the Presbyterian Church in America. The remains of James Grier, Nathaniel Irwin, John King, Robert Smith, John F. Grier, Robert White, William Latta, John Carmichael, Nathan Grier, and of many others, await the resurrection of the Just in the graveyards belonging to the congregations which were their only charge.

Such long-continued labor in the same portion of Zion, which Dr. A. Alexander correctly regarded as a strong proof of ministerial faithfulness, is well exemplified in the pastorate of the Rev. Dr. J. N. C. Grier. From his installation until weighed down by the burden of years he made known "the truth as it is in Jesus" from the pulpit of the same church. Surely much that is interesting and worthy of remembrance must have occurred in connection with him, and with the people among whom he "served God in the Gospel of his Son" for nearly sixty years. Shall the pages of history be crowded with the deeds of warriors and statesmen, and no place be found for even the names of those who have disseminated and impressed the precepts of that Holy Book, which are the sources of individual and national well-being?

John Nathan Caldwell, second son of the Rev. Nathan Grier, was born the 8th of June, 1792, on a farm in West Brandywine Township, then the property of his father, and now occupied by his daughter, Mrs. Louisa Parke. He received his classical education at the Brandywine Academy under the direction chiefly of the Rev. John F. Grier, and his collegiate at Dickinson College, Carlisle, Pa., where he was graduated in September, 1809. Shortly after his graduation he became the subject of Divine grace, and his thoughts being turned towards "the ministry of reconciliation," he began the study of theology in the school established for that purpose by his father. Having successfully applied himself to the prescribed preparation for a herald of righteousness, he was licensed to preach the Gospel by the Presbytery of New Castle on the 7th of April, 1813.

Mr. Grier passed the next year and a half as a probationer, supplying vacant pulpits within the bounds of the Presbytery, and after the death of his father, received a unanimous call to become his successor. This he accepted, and on the 24th of November, 1814, was ordained and installed by the Presbytery with which the Church had been long connected. On that occasion the Rev. Mr. Arthur, of Pequea, presided, and the Rev. Mr. Graham, of New London, preached the sermon.

With the example of his godly father to guide and animate, and the fervent prayers of the congregation that the mantle of the father might fall on the son, the youthful pastor entered on the discharge of the duties of his sacred office. But although he made known the great truths of the Gospel with earnestness and power, and there were manifest tokens of the divine approval of his labors, yet there was no general awakening until 1822, when forty-one were added to the membership of the Church.

This was followed by a dearth of spiritual blessings, but in 1831, seemingly in answer to the earnest wrestling with God in prayer by the members of the Presbytery of New Castle, there was a copious outpouring of the spirit.

Like the revival which began in Freehold, New Jersey, a century before, "this refreshing from the presence of the Lord" was not confined to this church in which its glorious effects first became manifest, but it extended to the neighboring congregations of all denominations. Under its blessed influence one hundred and twenty-seven were added in that year to the number worshipping here, and two hundred and thirty-three in the six years next following.

Owing to the large increase the meeting-house was crowded on the Sabbath. This was relieved to some extent in 1833 by the organization of a church at Coatesville, made up in part of those who had been connected with this congregation.

But in 1835, the number of members being nearly seven hundred, it became necessary either to enlarge the Meeting-House or to divide. After a discussion of the subject at several congregational meetings held for the purpose, it was finally resolved to separate. As a consequence of this determination a building was erected, and a church composed entirely of those who had been under the pastoral supervision of Dr. Grier was organized at Waynesburg, now Honeybrook. The large attendance was further reduced, in 1839, by the establishment of Fairview Presbyterian Church in Wallace Township.

Thus in the short period of seven years three Presbyterian Churches, which have grown and prospered, were organized by those a majority of whom had professed their faith in Christ, and united with the congregation worshipping in this place.

During the remainder of Dr. Grier's ministry, although there was no special manifestation of the Divine presence, there was an ingathering at every Communion season, and notwithstanding the organization of a church at Downingtown in 1863, the membership of his charge equalled that of fifty years before. The whole number received into the fellowship of the church during his pastorate being about thirteen hundred.

In addition to the preparation and delivery of upwards of five thousand sermons, the baptism of nearly one thousand infants and adults, pastoral visits, attendance on the sick, conducting the services at funerals, and Sunday-school superintendence, Dr. Grier took an active part in the temperance reformation, and frequently addressed the public on that subject. A determined foe of intemperance, no one did more to guard both the old and the young against its insidious advance than he who stood for more than half a century on the watch-tower of human welfare and happiness.

But the toil, the trials, and even the triumphs of his long ministry at last unfitted him for further labor in the Gospel field, and on the 14th of April, 1869, the pastoral relation was dissolved at his request* by the Presbytery of New Castle.

His work was done, but not until the children and many of the children's children of those to whom he first ministered, had been brought by his faithfulness to know "the God of their fathers, and to serve Him with a perfect heart and with a willing mind."

During the remainder of his sojourn on this side of Jordan, although enduring much bodily suffering, Dr. Grier patiently and prayerfully awaited the dividing of the waters, and on the 15th of September, 1880, entered the promised land,† to which all, except two, of those with whom he first met at the "table of the Lord," had preceded him. His death cast a gloom over the community, and a large number assembled to pay the last tribute of respect to him whom they had

---

* See Appendix I.

† He was the last survivor of those who prepared for the ministry under the direction of his father.

often seen, on a like occasion, standing beside the unclosed coffin or the newly-made grave, warning the impenitent or consoling the bereaved. The funeral services were conducted in the church. After some feeling remarks by the pastor, Mr. McColl, and the delivery of an impressive Commemorative Address by Dr. Bingham, of Oxford, Pa., the oldest of the sixteen clergymen present, the members of the congregation, and many besides, took leave of the remains. They were then borne by the most aged pastors in attendance to their last resting-place in the Upper Graveyard.

Dr. Grier firmly upheld what he believed to be right, was punctual in meeting his engagements, and aided the Councils of the Church, from which he was rarely absent, by his sound judgment and experience. He took a lively interest in the various religious institutions of his day, and every feasible plan for their extension received his cordial support.

His manner in the pulpit was earnest and solemn, and his plain, practical discourses, decidedly evangelical and pervaded by a tone of unaffected piety, "were blessed for the conversion of many."

No productions of his pen have appeared in print except a Historical Discourse delivered in 1849, and an Address to those who had assembled to congratulate him on the completion of the fiftieth year of his pastorate. In both of these publications, but especially in the last mentioned, many interesting occurrences of his ministry are given.

The degree of Doctor of Divinity was conferred on him by Washington College, Pa., in 1841.

Dr. Grier was united in marriage, on the 9th of September, 1813, to Nancy R., eldest daughter of Captain James Ralston, a leading member of his congregation. She died on the 7th of November, 1873, after having for more than sixty years contributed by her prudence, discretion, and piety to increase his means of usefulness and promote the beneficent operations of his charge. They had a family of four daughters: Susannah, the eldest, died while young; Louisa was married to Richard Parke, then a resident of Chester Valley; Frances to Thomas G. Happersett, late of Baltimore, Md.; and Agnes to G. Washington Neely, recently deceased, and long a resident of Ohio.*

---

* Minutes of Pres. of Newcastle; Dr. J. N. C. Grier, "Hist. Discourse;" Obituary Notice, by Rev. J. C. Thompson; by Rev. John McColl; Local Memoranda.

RULING ELDERS.

Ruling Elders being the governing body in a Presbyterian Church, and those on whose prudence, zeal, and piety the prosperity of a congregation largely depends, it might be supposed that at least their names and the time of their ordination could be ascertained by the Church Register. But, unfortunately, no records of Session during the first eighty years of the existence of this Church can be found. It is, therefore, impossible to state many things which it would be desirable to know respecting the godly men who upheld the hands of the pastors during that long period, and whose faithfulness may be traced in the growth and vigor of the Church.

The following list, gathered from a variety of sources, contains, it is believed, the names of nearly all who have been Ruling Elders since the organization of a Church in this place. But in regard to several of them the writer, after diligent inquiry, has been unable to learn the date of their ordination, and in some instances of their resignation or death.

Earliest Periods at which they are known to have been Ruling Elders.

1735.

Edward Irwin . . . . Died about 1750.
John Hamilton, ceased to act in 1741 . " in May, 1761.

IN "THE FORKS OF BRANDYWINE."

Robert Hamilton, ceased to act in 1741.
James Ward, ceased to act in 1741.

1741.

John Henderson, ceased to act in 1759.
Francis Alexander. . . . . Died in Aug., 1778.

1745.

Thomas Reese, M.D.
Matthew Robertson, resigned before 1760 . . Died July 30, 1792.

1760.

Samuel Allen, removed to Mercer County about 1805.
Thomas Brown.
William Brown . . . . Died in Jan., 1786.
John Culbertson . . . . " Sept. 2, 1794.
William Denny, Sr. . . . . " Oct. 8, 1784.
David Denny . . . . " Nov. 4, 1820.
Francis Gardner . . . . " in Sept., 1783.
William Ervin . . . . " Dec. 18, 1794.

1776.

Samuel Holliday, resigned in 1783.
Colonel Robert Smith . . . . Died in Dec., 1803.

1785.

William Hunter . . . . Died Dec. 18, 1804.
William Kennedy . . . . " Feb. 18, 1814.

1787.

Samuel Culbertson . . . . Died in April, 1788.

1801 or 1802.

John Robeson, resigned before 1814 . . . . Died Nov. 4, 1846.

1814.

Joseph Grier . . . . Died Nov. 10, 1830.

James Lockhart, resigned in 1829; removed in October, 1829, to the western part of Pennsylvania.
Richard Templin . . . . Died in Nov., 1824.
William Denny . . . . " Jan. 14, 1819.
Joseph M'Clure, Sr., resigned in 1825 . . . " Oct. 15, 1827.
James Ralston, Sr. . . . . " Jan. 28, 1834.

Ordained.
1815.

Matthew Stanley, resigned in 1840 . . . . Died June 15, 1844.
John Buchanan, resigned in 1837 . . . . " Aug. 22, 1856.
William Templeton . . . . " Sept. 1, 1849.
Robert Ralston . . . . " Aug. 14, 1844.

1825.

Dan Kirkpatrick . . . . Died Sept. 19, 1829.
John Templeton . . . . " July 27, 1865.
William Lockhart, resigned in 1829; removed in October, 1829, to the western part of Pennsylvania.
Robert McIntyre . . . . Died Feb. 18, 1844.
David Buchanan, resigned in 1835 . . . . " Feb. 20, 1875.

1830.

Samuel Ralston . . . . Died Jan. 1, 1859.
James H. Long . . . . " July 13, 1857.
Joseph M'Clure, resigned in 1839 . . . . " Nov. 11, 1861.
John M'Clure, resigned in 1839 . . . . . " Feb. 9, 1873.

1844.

John Ralston . . . . Died Apr. 21, 1880.
William N. Long . . . . " July 13, 1862.
David Williams . . . . " Feb. 7, 1849.
Caleb Liggett . . . . " March 2, 1876.

1859.

William Robeson . . . . Died Nov. 27, 1871.
James K. Grier . . . . " Jan. 8, 1867.

John Dauman . . . . . . Died Oct. 5, 1871.
Andrew Buchanan . . . . " Oct. 2, 1872.
James Liggett.

1869.

John F. Templeton, resigned in 1876.

1870.

Gordon Lallock, resigned in 1871.

1877.

Baxter B. M'Clure, resigned in 1882.
John Weber.
Nathan G. Thompson.
Benjamin Rea, resigned in 1883.

1882.

F. H. Irwin.
Charles T. Forrest.
Lewis Worrall.

Samuel Allen, Thomas Brown, William Brown, John Culbertson, William Denny, Sr., Francis Gardner, and Francis Alexander were members of the Session when Mr. Carmichael was installed.

William Denny, Sr., Francis Gardner, and Francis Alexander died during his pastorate; Samuel Holliday, who settled in the neighborhood in 1765, and Colonel Robert Smith were elders in 1776, and William Hunter, William Kennedy, David Denny, and Samuel Culbertson in 1787. It is, therefore, altogether likely that Samuel Culbertson, Samuel Allen, David Denny, William Hunter, William Irwin, Thomas Brown, and Colonel Robert Smith composed the bench of Elders when the Rev. Nathan Grier became pastor. But owing to removal, resignation, or death, all of them had ceased to be members of Session before Mr. Grier's decease.

When Dr. Grier was installed the Ruling Elders were James Lockhart, Richard Templin, James Ralston, Joseph Grier, William Denny, and Joseph McClure, Sr. During his pastorate he ordained twenty-one elders, and in the same period eighteen of those with whom he had taken such sweet counsel "in the household of faith" went to their graves in peace.

When Mr. Heberton became pastor the members of Session were John Ralston, Caleb Liggett, Andrew Buchanan, William Robeson, John Dauman, James Liggett, and John F. Templeton.

When he withdrew the members of Session were John Ralston, Caleb Liggett, James Liggett, and John F. Templeton.

The Ruling Elders at the present time are James Liggett, John Weber, Nathan G. Thompson, Lewis Worrall, Charles T. Forrest, and Frederick H. Irwin, all of whom, except James Liggett, have been ordained by Mr. McColl.

ADDITIONAL NOTICES.

Edward Irwin was among the first who settled in what is now West Brandywine Township. He was one of the Commissioners sent by the congregation in 1736 with the second call for Mr. Black. After the separation he attended the ministry of Mr. Boyd.

John Hamilton, Robert Hamilton, and James Ward took an active part in the organization of the church. They withdrew with the New Side in 1741, and perhaps were members of Session in Mr. Dean's congregation. John Hamilton was one of the witnesses to Mr. Dean's will.

John Henderson was a Ruling Elder in Mr. Boyd's church until 1757, which seems to have been the time of his decease.

Francis Alexander was a supporter of Mr. Boyd during the whole of his pastorate, and probably a member of Session.

Francis Gardner, a native of the North of Ireland, settled near the Beaver Dam, in Nantmeal, now Honeybrook Township, in 1733. He was a Ruling Elder a part of Mr. Boyd's and nearly the whole of Mr. Carmichael's pastorate. Like all the Scotch-Irish, Mr. Gardner was an active patriot during the struggle for national independence.

Matthew Robertson (Robeson), who died at the age of ninety-two, was upwards of half a century a faithful member of the church, and one of those to whom the land first owned by the congregation was patented by the heirs of Penn.

William Brown was a Ruling Elder more than a quarter of a century. His youngest daughter, Catharine, was married in 1776 to Dr. McMillan, and shared with him the trials and privations of life on the frontier, upwards of forty years.

Colonel Robert Smith was an active patriot during the Revolutionary War, sheriff of Chester County, a Justice of the Peace, and a member of the State Legislature in 1785.

William Hunter was a successful agent in collecting funds for restoring the Meeting-House after it had been destroyed by fire; a Justice of the Peace, and one of the executors of Mr. Carmichael's estate.

Joseph Grier was a lieutenant in the Continental Army, and one of the "Thirty Men" who were left to keep up the camp-fires, near Trenton, while the American army moved to the attack at Princeton.

John Culbertson, Esq., and David Denny were active in arresting the suspected, and did good service by forwarding supplies to the "Continental Army" and assisting the families of those in the field.

Matthew Stanley was a member of the State Legislature in 1829, '30, and many years a Justice of the Peace.

Robert Ralston held the office of Prothonotary during Governor Wolf's administration, 1829–'35. He took an active part in the organization of the Presbyterian Church at West Chester, and was one of its first Ruling Elders.

Andrew Buchanan was a member of the State Legislature in 1855, '56, and one of four brothers who were Ruling Elders in the Presbyterian Church.

A son of each of the following Ruling Elders entered the Gospel Ministry: William Kennedy, Joseph Grier, Samuel Ralston, John Templeton, and Caleb Liggett.

The fathers of the Ruling Elders whose names are subjoined were also Ruling Elders: William Denny, William Lockhart, David Buchanan, John McClure, Joseph McClure, John Ralston, Andrew Buchanan, John F. Templeton, and James Liggett.*

---

* Dr. Grier, "Historical Discourse;" Records of Session; Penna. Magazine; Local Memoranda; Office of Register of Wills.

TRUSTEES.

As it has been found impossible to obtain the names of many who held the office of Trustee, lists of them are given at those periods only when either their services being most needed, or some incidental circumstance caused their names to be placed on record.

The Trustees when the Manor Meeting-House was built, in 1761, were Rev. John Carmichael, John Culbertson, Esq., James Moore, Esq., William Denny, Samuel McKinly, and Francis Gardner.

When the Meeting-House was destroyed by fire, in 1786, those who, as Trustees, took an active part in its restoration were Samuel Cunningham, Esq., John Culbertson, Esq., James M'Clure, David Denny, James Dunwoodie, William Anderson, and Robert Lockhart.

In 1839, when the interior of the building was remodelled, John Templeton, Esq., John Ralston, James Dorlan, Thomas M'Clune, James K. Grier, William W. M'Clure, Joseph Mackelduff, and John M'Cachran composed the board of Trustees

James G. Templeton, Charles T. Forrest, John Weber, Lewis Worrall, James G. M'Clure, David Harris, Isaac Sahler, Zebulon W. Davis, and Baxter B. M'Clure held the office when the new church edifice was commenced in 1875. Three of them were the sons of those who were Trustees thirty-six years before.

The Trustees at the present time are James G. M'Clure, Charles A. Robeson, W. P. Moore, Charles T. Forrest, Zebulon W. Davis, Joseph P. Graham, Robert Shields, Samuel C. Mackelduff, and Francis Growe.

SEXTONS.

The Sextons, so far as can be ascertained, have been John M'Cachran, Isabella M'Cachran, James Neal, James Millegan, Sr., James Millegan, Jr., Joseph Sims, Samuel Parsons, John Sinn, Griffith Sinn, William Ballentine, and Robert Cairns.*

---

* Local Memoranda; Sessional Records in part.

THEOLOGICAL STUDENTS.

"How beautiful upon the mountains are the feet of him that bringeth good tidings, that publisheth peace, that bringeth good tidings of good, that publisheth salvation."—Isaiah lii. 7.

Those whose names are appended prepared for the Christian Ministry under the direction of the Rev. Nathan Grier. The Biographical notices of them have been arranged in the order of their license to preach the Gospel.*

Rev. William Woods	Licensed in	June, 1794.
" David M'Conaughy, D.D., LL.D.	"	" Oct., 1797.
" Patrick Davidson	"	" Oct., 1797.
" Matthew G. Wallace	"	" April, 1799.
" Thomas Grier	"	" April, 1800.
" Joshua Knight	"	" Oct., 1800.
" Thomas Hood	"	" Aug., 1802.
" Levi Bull, D.D.	"	" Sept., 1805.
" Alexander Boyd	"	" Sept., 1806.
" James Buchanan	"	" Sept., 1806.
" Robert White	"	" April, 1809.
" William Kennedy	"	" April, 1809.
" John F. Grier, D.D.	"	" June, 1810.
" Robert S. Grier	"	" Sept., 1812.
" Samuel Parke	"	" April, 1813.
" John H. Grier	"	" April, 1813.
" John N. C. Grier, D.D.	"	" April, 1813.
" John W. Grier	"	" Sept., 1818.

* Minutes of Pres. of Newcastle.

REV. WILLIAM WOODS.

The Rev. William Woods, who appears to have been the first that pursued his Theological studies under the direction of the Rev. Nathan Grier, was a native of Lancaster County, Pa. His academical education was obtained at Dr. Smith's school in Pequea, and his collegiate at Dickinson College, of which he became an Alumnus in 1792. He was licensed by the Presbytery of New Castle, June 17, 1794, and spent some years after his licensure as a missionary in the western counties of this State.

Mr. Woods accepted a call from the united churches of Bethel and Lebanon, in Alleghany County, Pa., as the successor of the Rev. John Clark, and was installed as their pastor by the Presbytery of Redstone, June 28, 1797. The pastoral relation was dissolved in 1831, and he died October 17, 1834.

Bethel, of which Mr. Woods became sole pastor some years before his death, was organized by Dr. McMillan, and is one of the oldest churches in Western Pennsylvania. "It shared largely in the blessed influences of the revivals of 1803–'04."[*]

---

[*] Smith, "Old Redstone;" Minutes of Presbytery of Newcastle.

REV. DAVID M'CONAUGHY, D.D., LL.D.

Rev. David M'Conaughy, D.D., LL.D., was born in Adams County, then a part of York County, Pa., in September, 1775. He was graduated at Dickinson College, Carlisle, September 30, 1795, standing the first in his class. After the usual course in Theology under the direction of the Rev. Nathan Grier, he was licensed by the Presbytery of New Castle, October 5, 1797.

Having received a call from the united congregations of Upper Marsh Creek (now Gettysburg) and Great Conewago, he was installed as their pastor in October, 1800. He continued in this relation, faithfully and acceptably discharging his ministerial duties, until the spring of 1832, when the pastoral relation was dissolved at his request.

In May, 1832, he was inaugurated President of Washington College, Pa., an office which he filled with dignity and ability until October, 1849, when the infirmities of age caused him to resign. He continued to reside at Washington until his death, January 29, 1852.

Dr. M'Conaughy was an early and zealous advocate of the temperance cause, and his influence, both as a pastor and as the President of a college, was widespread and beneficial. He left the congregations committed to his oversight in a prosperous condition, and "every year of his administration added strength and reputation to Washington College."

After his retirement from the Presidency, Dr. M'Conaughy published a volume of Discourses, chiefly Biographical, of Persons eminent in Sacred History; a Brief Summary and Outline of the Principal Subjects comprehended in Moral Science; a few Baccalaureate Addresses, and some Sermons.

His style is generally vigorous, although somewhat diffuse, and his writings exhibit clearness in the statement of facts, a judicious selection of the subjects discussed, and an earnest desire to promote knowledge and religion.

The degree of D.D. was conferred on him by Jefferson College in 1833; of LL.D. by the Trustees of Washington College on his retirement from the Presidency of that Institution.*

REV. PATRICK DAVIDSON.

Patrick Davidson was born in 1775, and completed his collegiate course at Dickinson College, Carlisle, September 30, 1795.† He was licensed by the Presbytery of New Castle, October 5, 1797, and passed the next twelve months in supplying churches without a pastor.

In April, 1798, Mr. Davidson received a call from

---

* Dr. Nevin, "Churches of the Valley;" Sprague, "Annals of American Pulpit;" Rev. Dr. Elliott's Com. Discourse.

† Among his classmates were Chief Justice Taney, Judge Kennedy, of the Supreme Court of this State, Dr. McConaughy, President of Washington College, and Dr. Williams, President of Jefferson College.

the congregation of Fagg's Manor, Chester County, Pa., which he declined on account of the smallness of the salary. The call, accompanied by a promise of increased support, was renewed at the meeting of Presbytery in October of the same year, and accepted.

He was installed in April, 1799, and remained about a year. He then applied for a release from his charge, alleging "that although the congregation had done all that was reasonable, yet certain unpleasant circumstances had occurred which destroyed his comfort and hindered his usefulness."

The Presbytery granted his request, and on the 19th of October, 1800, he was installed pastor of the church at Toms Creek, Maryland, by a committee of the Presbytery of Carlisle. In 1801 he also became pastor of the church at Piney Creek in the same State, giving to each of these churches one-half of his time.

His pastoral relation with both congregations seems to have been harmonious and pleasant until the close of the summer of 1809. In August (15th) of the same year he was elected Principal of the Academy at Fredericktown, Md., and removed there shortly afterwards. This caused dissatisfaction among his people, who complained that the preaching of the Word was neglected, and at the meeting of Presbytery in the Spring of 1810, they asked for supplies. Mr. Davidson being absent, the Presbytery deferred action until its meeting the next September (26th), when the pastoral relation was dissolved.

At the same meeting of Presbytery a number of charges against Mr. Davidson were presented by a member of one of his congregations. A Committee of Presbytery, after a careful examination, considered them unfounded and censured his accuser.

He was dismissed at his own request on the 25th of September, 1814, to the Presbytery of Baltimore. During his connection with the Academy at Fredericktown "he supplied the Presbyterian Church at that place, and preached occasionally at Pipe Creek and Creagertown in the vicinity."

Mr. Davidson died October 9, 1824. He was the first that was called to his reward of those who entered the ministry from the Divinity School of the Rev. Nathan Grier.*

REV. MATTHEW G. WALLACE.

The Rev. M. G. Wallace was born about the year 1774. Where he received his academical training is not known. He was graduated at the College of New Jersey in September, 1795, and succeeded the Rev. Mr. McPherson as principal of the Brandywine Academy, where he remained about three years. While he had charge of the Academy he pursued the study of Theology, and was licensed by the Presbytery of Newcastle, April 4, 1799. He removed immediately afterwards to Ohio, and was one of the first Presbyterian ministers who settled in that State.

---

* Minutes of Presbytery of Carlisle; Rev. W. Simonton, "History of Toms Creek Church;" Rev. W. Noble, "History of Fagg's Manor Church."

About 1802, Mr. Wallace became pastor of the First Presbyterian Church in Cincinnati. Subsequently he preached at Springfield, Hamilton, and other places in Ohio. In the latter part of his life he resided at Terre Haute, Ind., without a charge, and died there August 12, 1854.

Mr. Wallace was an excellent classical scholar, a sound theologian, and a faithful minister of the Gospel.*

REV. THOMAS GRIER.

Middletown, the oldest, and for nearly a century and a half the only, Presbyterian Church in what is now Delaware County, Pa., was established before 1724. It seems to have been among the first organized outside of Philadelphia. As the records are lost, its early history is obscure. A copy, however, of Watts's Psalms and Hymns, presented to the church by the author, has escaped the ravages of time, and is justly regarded as an interesting memento of that eminent and godly man.

In the latter half of the first year of the present century the congregation known by the name of Middletown presented a call to the Rev. Thomas Grier to become their pastor. This call he accepted, and was ordained and installed December 16, 1801.

Mr. Grier was graduated at Dickinson College in 1797, studied divinity under the Rev. Nathan Grier,

---

* Dr. S. Alexander, "Princeton College in the Eighteenth Century;" "Reminiscences of Rev. Dr. J. N. C. Grier."

and was licensed by the Presbytery of Newcastle, April 3, 1800.

He remained at Middletown until the close of September (30th), 1808, when he resigned and accepted a call from the church at West Town, Orange County, New York, in the bounds of the Presbytery of Hudson.

Of his pastorate at Middletown little is known; but taking his subsequent ministry as a guide, it may be inferred that it was faithful, laborious, and successful.

He was installed at West Town, February 7, 1809. The bounds of the congregation were large, embracing the territory now occupied by four churches. He labored with great diligence and acceptance until difficulties arose with some of the members of his charge on the subject of baptism. The matter was finally brought to the notice of the Presbytery, and in April (18th), 1827, the whole matter was referred to a Committee, which accepted his resignation in September (12th) of the same year.

Shortly afterwards Mr. Grier became pastor of the church at Milford, Pike County, Pa., and remained about a year. He then settled at Centreville, N. J., where a meeting-house was built for him. After a pastorate of nearly three years in that place, he removed to Cold Spring, on the Hudson, where he continued to occupy the pulpit until his death.

"He was taken sick while preaching from the text, 'Weep not for me, but weep for yourselves and your children.'"

Mr. Grier preached without the aid of notes, and

with such earnestness and solemnity as frequently to melt his audience to tears. His sermons were practical, sound in doctrine, and imbued with much of the spirit of his Divine Master. His labors, especially during his pastorate at West Town, were greatly blessed.

In 1815 there was a copious outpouring of the Spirit among the people of his charge, one hundred and three being added to the church in that year, and fifty-seven in the year immediately following; all on a profession of their faith. In 1820 a still greater awakening took place, and a hundred and ninety-four became members of the visible church.

Mr. Grier married a Miss McCullough, of Little Britain, Lancaster County, Pa., and one of his sons, George W. Grier, resides in Goshen, Orange County, N. Y.*

REV. JOSHUA KNIGHT.

About the middle of the last century a number of Presbyterian families associated together and emigrated from Connecticut to Southwestern Central New York. They purchased a quarter township of land, and settled on the Chenango River, a tributary of the Susquehanna, near where the town of Sherburne now stands. They arrived on Thursday, and by the next Sabbath they had built a log meeting-house, in which divine service was held every week. This building

---

* Com. from Rev. T. Sheelar, Orange Co., N. Y.; Smith, "Hist. of Delaware Co.;" Minutes of Presbytery of Hudson.

having in the course of time become no longer fit for public worship, they determined to erect another. A difference of opinion, however, about the site of the new meeting-house led to a division. A part of the congregation withdrew, organized as a second church, and built a house at some distance from the town.

In 1802 the Rev. Joshua Knight, a graduate of Dickinson College in 1798, and a licentiate of the Presbytery of Newcastle in 1800, was installed pastor of this church. He discharged the duties of the office with acceptance until 1823. In that year he married the daughter of his first wife, step-daughter, and as a consequence was deposed from the ministry by the Congregational Association of Chenango County. He removed shortly afterwards from Sherburne to a farm belonging to his wife on the Mohawk River, in Herkimer County, where he spent some years in agriculture. He subsequently engaged in mercantile pursuits, but his property having been destroyed by fire, he was reduced to penury. His wife died of grief, and he, after having, as reported, officiated as a Universalist clergyman, closed his earthly existence as a pauper.

That the evening of a life whose morning and noon were passed prosperously and respectably should have been clouded by poverty and disgrace, gives rise to many sad and monitory reflections. But the duty of the biographer is the stating of facts, not the penning of meditations on the errors and frailties of humanity.

His children by the last marriage all died when young. A son by his first marriage, it is said, resides in Michigan.

The second church at Sherburne was small, never numbering more than two hundred members. It shared largely in the revival of 1816. In 1830 it disbanded and formed another organization in a village five miles distant.*

REV. THOMAS HOOD.

Thomas Hood was born on the farm now in the possession of the family of the late Matthew Stanly, July 2, 1781. He was awakened to a sense of his lost condition by the preaching of the Rev. Nathan Grier. After he had been connected for some time with Mr. Grier's congregation, he determined to enter the ministry. His preparatory training was received at the Brandywine Academy, and his collegiate at Dickinson College, where he was graduated in September, 1799. He was licensed by the Presbytery of Newcastle, August 3, 1802, and spent about three years as an occasional supply in the central counties of this State.

In October, 1805, Mr. Hood was installed by the Presbytery of Huntingdon pastor of the united congregations of Buffalo and Washington, in Northumberland, now Union, County, Pa. At first he gave to each of these congregations half his time. But the congregation at Washington having been

---

* New York Hist. Collections; Hotchkin's "Hist. of Western New York;" MS. Com. from Rev. J. Chambers, Pastor of Cong. Church, Sherburne.

reduced by the change of residence of many of its members, they consented, in 1809, to an agreement for Mr. Hood to preach there every fourth Sabbath.

At a meeting of the Presbytery held at Bellefonte in 1810, the residents of Milton and vicinity, in Northumberland County, requested permission for Mr. Hood to preach for them one-fourth of his time. This request was granted by the recently-formed Presbytery of Northumberland, and he conducted religious services at Milton once a month as a stated supply until October 7, 1812, when he was installed as pastor.

On the 20th of April, 1819, he accepted an invitation to give the congregation at Milton one-half of his time. "This arrangement continued until he resigned the pastorate, April 21, 1835." Mr. Hood was noted for the excellence and solidity of his matter rather than for elegant diction or an attractive delivery.

After his withdrawal from the active duties of the ministry, Mr. Hood resided for some years on his farm in Buffalo Valley, Union County, but he finally removed to Lewisburg, the seat of justice of the same county, where he died March 17, 1848.

He was married in April, 1803, to Miss Mary Hazlitt. His second wife was Miss Hannah M'Clure, to whom he was married in March, 1848, a short time before his decease.*

---

* Com. from Rev. J. C. Wattson, D.D.; "Hist. of Presbytery of Huntingdon;" "Reminiscences of Ex-Governor Pollock."

REV. LEVI BULL, D.D.

The Rev. Levi Bull was born in Warwick, then a part of East Nantmeal Township, Chester County, November 14, 1780. He manifested an aptitude for learning at an early age, and was graduated at Dickinson College in September, 1798, before he had completed his eighteenth year.

He commenced the study of Law in the office of James Hopkins, Esq., Lancaster, Pa., but before he was admitted to the Bar his religious opinions underwent a change, and he resolved to devote himself to the service of the Altar. With this object in view he passed through the usual theological course in the Divinity School of the Rev. Nathan Grier, entered the ministry of the Episcopal Church, and was ordained by Bishop White in 1805.

Instead of seeking a rectorship at a distance, he devoted himself to the preaching of the Gospel in the vicinity of his native place. His earnestness and faithfulness, together with his popular manners, caused his ministrations to be largely attended, and resulted in the organization of several Episcopal Churches, which still exist.*

The possessor of ample means both by inheritance and marriage, Dr. Bull generously assisted every benevolent object, and the deserving poor never sought

---

* Dr. Bull was rector in 1833 of St. Mary's Church, Warwick Township, Chester County; Bangor Church, Churchtown, Lancaster County; and St. Thomas' Church, Morgantown, Berks County.

his aid in vain. Imbued by a truly Christian philanthropy, he regarded ministers of the Gospel of every orthodox denomination as his brethren, and mingled freely with men of every creed. He is the only Episcopal clergyman whom the writer remembers to have seen occupying a Presbyterian pulpit. At his death, which took place August 2, 1859, he was the oldest rector of the Episcopal Church in Pennsylvania. The degree of D.D. was conferred on him in 1844 by the Western University of Pennsylvania, located at Pittsburg.

The father of Dr. Bull, Colonel Thomas Bull, was a soldier in the "Continental Army;"* a Representative from Chester County in the State Legislature nine sessions, 1793 to 1801 inclusive, and a delegate to the Convention which framed the Constitution of Pennsylvania, adopted in 1776.

The eldest son of Dr. Bull, Colonel Thomas K. Bull, a gentleman of liberal education and pleasing address, resides on the paternal estate. He was a member of the State Legislature three years,—1846, '47, and '48. Another son, James, held the office of Prosecuting Attorney for Chester County, and a third son, William, recently deceased, was a member of the Philadelphia Bar.

A grandson of Dr. Bull, the Rev. Levi Bull, is a rector in the Episcopal Church.

* Colonel Bull was among those taken prisoners by the surrender of Fort Washington in November, 1776, and endured all the privations and sufferings of that Libby of the Revolutionary War, the British prison-ship. He is said to have broken his sword rather than surrender it.

A discourse commemorative of Dr. Bull was delivered by the Rev. Dr. May in 1859.*

REV. ALEXANDER BOYD.

Alexander Boyd, a native of Cumberland County, Pa., was born about 1780. When quite young he removed to the vicinity of Pittsburg, and prosecuted his academical studies at Cannonsburg, before Jefferson College was founded. His collegiate course was completed at Dickinson College in 1799.

Having spent some years in teaching, and passed through the usual course in Theology under the direction of the Rev. Nathan Grier, he was licensed by the Presbytery of Newcastle, September 30, 1806. In 1808 he was installed pastor of the church in Bedford, Pa., by the Presbytery of Carlisle. After laboring there about eight years he accepted a call from the Presbyterian Church at Newtown, Bucks County, where he was installed by the Presbytery of Philadelphia in 1817. Owing to a difference of views between him and a number of the leading members of his congregation on the subject of temperance, he resigned his charge at Newtown, in 1838, and settled at Lock Haven, Clinton County, Pa. He remained there until a year before his death, which occurred in 1845.

Mr. Boyd "was a man of faithfulness, prayer, and power," and left an impression on the community at

---

* Futhey, "Notæ Cestriensis;" May, Com. Discourse; Communication from Colonel T. Bull.

Newtown which is not yet effaced. During his Pastorate the congregation was blessed with several revivals, and not a year passed without the addition of members to the church, and many of them on a profession of their faith.

Mr. Boyd was twice married. His first wife was Miss Margaret Watson, daughter of Dr. John Watson, of Lancaster County. His second wife was Miss Ann Beatty, daughter of Dr. Reading Beatty, of Bucks County.*

REV. JAMES BUCHANAN.

The Rev. Mr. Buchanan was a native of Sadsbury Township, Chester County, Pa., where he was born in 1783. He received his academical training at the Brandywine Academy, and his collegiate at Dickinson College, where he was graduated September 28, 1803. Having completed his theological course, he was licensed by the Presbytery of Newcastle, September 30, 1806.

In April, 1809, he was installed as pastor of the united congregations of Harrisburg and Middle Paxton, where he labored about six years with "faithfulness and success." Failing health having compelled him to resign his charge, he spent some time in travelling. His health having been in a measure restored, he accepted a call in 1816 from the Presbyterian Church at Greencastle, Franklin County, Pa. He

---

* Com. from Rev. J. C. Bush, of Newtown, Pa.; Com. from Rev. Dr. Watson, of Milton, Pa.; Minutes of Northumberland Presbytery.

sustained this relation upwards of twenty years, when, owing to ill-health and a belief that a change of place would be beneficial both to himself and the people of his charge, he resigned, and became pastor of a church at Logansport, Indiana. He remained in connection with it until his death, in September, 1843.

Mr. Buchanan was much beloved by the members of the congregations of which he was pastor, and was highly esteemed by his brethren in the ministry.

Dr. Elliott, who knew him well, states in a biographical notice of him that his sermons in their structure were neat, systematic, and short; in their matter solid, evangelical, and practical; and in their manner grave, solemn, and earnest.*

REV. ROBERT WHITE.

Robert White was born in Montgomery County, Pa., in 1783. He pursued his preparatory studies at Norristown, and was licensed to preach by the Presbytery of Newcastle, April 4, 1809.

Shortly after his licensure calls were placed in his hands from Upper Octoraro, Fagg's Manor, and the united congregations of White Clay Creek and head of Christiana. He accepted the call from Fagg's Manor, and was ordained and installed December 14, 1809. He continued to be the pastor of that church until his death, in September, 1835.

His sermons were plain and practical, sound in

* Dr. Nevin, " Churches of the Valley;" Rev. David Elliott, D.D.

doctrine, and delivered in an earnest, impressive manner. Mr. White was well acquainted with history in general, and he frequently drew illustrations of the Providence of God from the records of the past which were both apt and striking.

The only production from the pen of Mr. White, which the writer has seen, is a sermon entitled " Melchisedek," delivered August 11, 1814. In it he advances the opinion that Job and Melchisedek were the same person. His views are well sustained, and the whole discourse is, perhaps, as clear an exposition as can be given of a subject from which the veil of mystery cannot be removed.

Mr. White married, in 1809, Nancy, eldest daughter of his theological preceptor, the Rev. Nathan Grier. Both of the sons of Mr. White entered the ministry.

The eldest, Nathan Grier White, after finishing his theological course at Princeton, was licensed by the Presbytery of Newcastle, October 2, 1833. He was ordained and installed pastor of the church at McConnelsburg, Bedford, now Fulton, County, Pa., June 11, 1834, a relation which he sustained "until the fall of 1864, when he accepted a call to Williamsburg, Blair County, Pa., where he is now laboring."

The younger, Robert M. White, was graduated at Amherst College in 1834, standing the second in his class. Having completed his theological course in 1837, he was ordained and installed pastor of the church at Fairview, West Virginia, in the autumn of that year.

In September, 1848, he became the pastor of the

Presbyterian Church of Chartiers, Washington County, Pa. But his ministry there was short. He died on the 14th of December, 1848.

A daughter, now deceased, of Mr. White was married to the Rev. John Moore. Another passed several years as a missionary in Northern India with her husband, the late Rev. Robert S. Fullerton.*

REV. WILLIAM KENNEDY.

William Kennedy, whose father was many years a Ruling Elder of the congregation worshipping in this place, was born July 4, 1783. Through the influence of his pious parents, aided by the faithful and earnest admonitions of his pastor, Rev. Nathan Grier, he was brought to a knowledge of the saving truths of the Gospel, and finally led to devote himself to the ministry of Reconciliation. He received his preparatory training at the Brandywine Academy, and having passed the usual time in the study of Theology under the direction of the Rev. Nathan Grier, was licensed April 6, 1809, by the Presbytery of Newcastle. On the 3d of October in the following year he was ordained and installed pastor of the united congregations of Lewistown and West Kishacoquillas, Pa., by the Presbytery of Huntingdon.

In April, 1822, charges were brought against him of conduct unbecoming a clergyman. These charges

---

* Futhey, "Notæ Cestriensis;" Rev. W. F. Noble, "Hist. of Pres. Church of Fagg's Manor;" Rev. J. F. Collier, "Hist. of Chartiers Church."

the Presbytery considered unsustained, but he was induced as a consequence to resign his pastorate.

"On the first of October, 1822, Mr. Kennedy was dismissed at his own request to the Presbytery of Erie, but finally settled within the bounds of the Presbytery of Clarion."

He supplied the congregation of Mount Tabor, in Jefferson County, and of Mill Creek, in Clarion County, until a short time before his death, which took place November 2, 1850.

Mr. Kennedy married, in 1809, Mary, third daughter of Benjamin McClure, an active member of this Church, and many years the leader of the choir. Four of their children, two sons and two daughters, reside within a short distance of Brookville, Jefferson County.

In regard to the charges which were preferred against Mr. Kennedy, it is no more than just to state that his contemporaries believed him to be a good and godly man, and that his subsequent lengthened ministry "was without suspicion and without reproach."*

REV. JOHN F. GRIER, D.D.

John Ferguson Grier, only son of the Rev. James Grier, of Deep Run, Bucks County, Pa., was born in 1784. He received his preparatory training at the Academy in this place, entered Dickinson College,

---

* Gibson, "Hist. of Huntingdon Presbytery;" Com. from William B. Kennedy; Minutes of Presbytery of Newcastle.

Carlisle, in 1799, and was graduated in 1803, at the head of his class. He subsequently taught in Pequea, was principal nearly five years of the Brandywine Academy, completed his Theological course under the direction of his uncle, the Rev. Nathan Grier, and was licensed to preach the Gospel by the Presbytery of Newcastle, June 26, 1810.

Dr. Grier settled at Reading, Pa., where he was instrumental in gathering together and organizing the First Presbyterian Church in that city, of which he was installed pastor November 23, 1814. In addition to the conscientious discharge of his pastoral duties he conducted a Classical School, which obtained a high reputation and was well patronized. A warm friend of education, he was several years an active Trustee of Dickinson College, and it is altogether likely if his life had been prolonged that the College would have remained under Presbyterian control. The honorary degree of D.D. was conferred on him by the College at Meadville.

Dr. Grier's manner in the pulpit was dignified and solemn, but close attention to his manuscript during the delivery of his sermons, which were models of diction and close thought, made them less attractive and impressive than their excellence merited.

He died suddenly, January 26, 1829, during the progress of a revival which added many to the membership of the church of which he had been the faithful and only pastor.*

---

* Sprague, "Annals of American Pulpit;" C. B. Penrose, Esq., Commemorative Discourse.

REV. ROBERT S. GRIER.

The eldest son of the Rev. Nathan Grier, Robert Smith Grier, was born May 11, 1790. In answer, no doubt, to the prayers of his godly parents, he was hopefully converted at an early age, and led to devote himself to the divinely-appointed work of winning souls to Christ.

Mr. Grier passed, from 1802 to 1807, in preparatory studies at the Brandywine Academy, and in the last-mentioned year entered Dickinson College, where he was graduated September 27, 1809. He studied Theology under the direction of his father, and was licensed by the Presbytery of Newcastle in September, 1812.

He preached as a supply to congregations without a pastor until the winter of 1814, when he received a call from the churches of Toms Creek, now Emmittsburg, and Piney Creek, Md. This call he accepted, and was ordained and installed by the Presbytery of Carlisle, November 14, 1814. He remained in the pastoral charge of these congregations until his death, on the 28th of December, 1865, closed his pastorate of fifty-one years.

The Christian fellowship which subsisted between Mr. Grier and the members of the churches of which he had the spiritual oversight is shown by his long residence among them, and his faithfulness, by the number gathered into the fold at each communion season. In the sanctuary, his manner was earnest and solemn, his language plain and direct, and his discourses argumentative, practical, and convincing.

It is worthy of remark that both the sons of the Rev. Nathan Grier, and also his sons-in-law, the Rev. Messrs. White and Parke, remained during the entire period of their ministry in charge of the congregations over which they were first installed. Like the pastor of Goldsmith's "Deserted Village,"

" Remote from towns, each ran his godly race,
And never changed, nor wished to change his place."

Both the sons of Robert S. Grier entered the ministry, and are laboring with acceptance in West Virginia. The elder, Smith F. Grier, as pastor of the New Cumberland Presbyterian Church, where the twenty-fifth anniversary of his installation has recently been celebrated, and the younger, Lafferty Grier, as pastor of the Elm Grove Presbyterian Church, where he has been stationed the last eighteen years.[*]

REV. SAMUEL PARKE.

Samuel Parke was born in Sadsbury Township, Chester County, November 25, 1788. His parents being members of the Upper Octoraro Church, he was early brought to a sense of his lost condition, and having experienced a change of heart, resolved to devote himself to the work of the Gospel Ministry.

---

[*] Rev. W. Simonton, "Hist. of Emmittsburg Pres. Church;" Minutes of Presbytery of Carlisle.

After careful preparation, he entered Dickinson College, Carlisle, and was graduated in September, 1809. Having completed his theological course, he was licensed by the Presbytery of Newcastle, April 7, 1813.

In August, 1814, Mr. Parke was ordained and installed Pastor of the Presbyterian Church of Slate Ridge, York County, Pa., and also of Centre Church in the same County, giving to the latter one-third of his time. He ministered to both of these congregations about thirty years, when he resigned the Pastorate of the Centre Church, but continued to occupy the pulpit of the Slate Ridge Church.

In 1857 the infirmities of age led him to obtain a dissolution of the Pastoral relation, and he remained without a charge until his death, December 20, 1869.

Mr. Parke faithfully performed the duties of his sacred office, and was much beloved by the members of his flock. During his ministry of more than forty years there were many tokens of the Divine approval of his labors, and the congregations of which he had the oversight annually increased. His manner in the pulpit was peculiarly solemn and impressive. Practical piety rather than doctrinal controversy formed the chief subject of his discourses.

Mr. Parke married Martha, the second daughter of the Rev. Nathan Grier.

His son, the Rev. Nathan Grier Parke, D.D., was graduated at Jefferson College in 1840, completed his theological course at Princeton in 1844, and is now Pastor of the Presbyterian Church at Pittston, Luzerne County, Pa.

In 1867, Dr. Parke, with others, represented the Old School Presbyterian Church in the Assembly of the Free Church of Scotland, and also in the United Presbyterian Church of the same country.*

REV. JOHN H. GRIER.

John Hays Grier, the eldest son of John and Jane (Hays) Grier, was born about seven miles from Doylestown, Bucks County, Pa., February 7, 1788. When he was quite young, his parents, who were members of the Deep Run Presbyterian Church, removed from Bucks County and settled on the farm recently owned by their grandson, Elder Baxter B. McClure.

Mr. Grier received his preparatory training at the Brandywine Academy, and completed his collegiate course at Dickinson College, Carlisle, in September, 1809. Among his classmates were James Buchanan, late President of the United States, Robert S. Grier, John W. Grier, and J. N. C. Grier, well-known ministers of the Gospel.

Mr. Grier studied Theology under the direction of his uncle, the Rev. Nathan Grier, and was licensed to preach the Gospel by the Presbytery of Newcastle, April 7, 1813. He was installed pastor of the United Churches of Pine Creek and Great Island, Lycoming County, Pa., in the Fall of 1814. He continued in charge of both these churches until 1827,

---

* Futhey, "Hist. of Upper Oct. Church;" Minutes of Presbytery of Carlisle; *Presbyterian Banner*.

when he resigned the pastorate of Great Island, now Lock Haven, and divided the time previously devoted to it between a charge in Nipenose Valley and another at New Berry, now included in the town of Williamsport.

In 1840 the members of the Pine Creek Church built a house for public worship in the village of Jersey Shore, and the congregation was afterwards designated by the name of that village, the term Pine Creek being dropped.

Mr. Grier resigned the pastorate of Jersey Shore in 1848, but continued to supply the congregation in Nipenose Valley until 1863, when he withdrew from the active duties of the ministry.

When he commenced his labors in Lycoming County it was sparsely settled, church buildings were few, and the opportunities for hearing the preached Word limited. At the close of his half-century of ministerial work the county was populous, churches were largely multiplied, and a band of devoted men, representing all the orthodox denominations, proclaimed the words of truth in cities and villages, occupying places where he had declared "the whole counsel of God" in an almost unbroken wilderness.

Unassuming and genial, Mr. Grier was always deservedly popular with the young people, not only of his charge but also of other denominations. This is evident from the fact that he solemnized a greater number of marriages than any other clergyman within the bounds of the Presbytery, being frequently called a distance of several miles to perform the interesting ceremony.

After the dissolution of the pastoral relation Mr. Grier resided at Jersey Shore. He was probably the oldest Presbyterian clergyman in this State, and, although his physical and mental powers were somewhat impaired, he entered on his ninetieth year in the enjoyment of comparatively good health.*

Mr. Grier died February 3, 1880, within four days of having completed his ninety-second year.

REV. JOHN W. GRIER.

John Walker Grier was born in Bucks County, Pa., in 1789. When he was quite young his parents removed from Bucks County and settled within the bounds of this congregation, of which his father, Colonel Jos. Grier, was upwards of twenty years a Ruling Elder.

Having been hopefully converted during a season of refreshing in the church, Mr. Grier, in obedience to his own sense of duty and the wishes of his pious parents, resolved to devote himself to the work of the Christian ministry. With this object in view, he passed through a preparatory course at the Brandywine Academy and entered Dickinson College, where he was graduated in 1809. His theological studies were commenced in the Divinity School of his uncle, the Rev. Nathan Grier, and completed under the direction of Dr. Mason, of New York City, and in the Seminary at Princeton, N. J.

Mr. Grier then turned his attention to teaching,

* Com. from R. H. Grier; Min. Pres. of Newcastle; Personal Reminiscences.

reopened the Brandywine Academy, which had been closed since the withdrawal of Dr. J. F. Grier, and continued in charge of it until the Spring of 1822, when he resigned, and became principal of the Chester County Academy. He retained his connection with that Institution until 1826, when he was appointed by John Quincy Adams a Chaplain in the navy of the United States. This office his amiable disposition, gentlemanly manners, and uniformly Christian deportment eminently qualified him to fill, and he discharged its duties to the satisfaction of all.

He held the position until 1857, when the infirmities of nearly threescore and ten caused him to resign, and he passed the remaining seven years of his life in literary leisure and the enjoyment of the society of his numerous friends.

During his connection with the navy, Mr. Grier visited nearly all of the commercial cities and many of the most interesting localities in both hemispheres; and his stores of information gathered during his voyages and travels made his conversation highly interesting and instructive. He was an excellent Hebraist, a good classical scholar, and a well-read theologian.

Mr. Grier was one of a Committee of eight who, in 1831, signed, in behalf of an association formed for the purpose, the contract for the publication of the first number of that widely-known and influential periodical the *Presbyterian*. He was also the first superintendent of the Manor Sunday-School.

Mr. Grier was licensed by the Presbytery of Newcastle, September 30, 1818, and ordained in 1826 by the Presbytery of Philadelphia, when he was about to enter the navy.

His only surviving son, the Rev. Matthew B. Grier, D.D., well known as the senior editor of the *Presbyterian*, was licensed by the Presbytery of Newcastle at Wilmington, Del., in 1843, and ordained and installed pastor of the Presbyterian Church at Ellicott's Mills, Md., by the Presbytery of Baltimore, in November, 1847.

The pastoral relation was dissolved at his request in November, 1852, and he accepted a call to the First Presbyterian Church, Wilmington, N. C. Dr. Grier remained at Wilmington, laboring faithfully and acceptably, until the outbreak of the Rebellion, when he was forced, on account of his loyalty to the Union, to withdraw to a Northern city. He has now been for many years the leading editor of the *Presbyterian*, and is at present supplying the church at Ridley Park, near the city of Philadelphia.*

The following members of his Congregation became Ministers of the Gospel during the Pastorate of Dr. J. N. C. Grier:

Rev. Robert M'Cachran.
" Anderson B. Quay.
" Britton E. Collins.
" Benjamin M. Nyce.
" Richard Walker.
" Matthew B. Grier, D.D.
" Rees Happersett, D.D.

Rev. Jas. G. Ralston, D.D., LL.D.
" William Pinkerton.
" William H. Templeton.
" John C. Thompson.
" John Pinkerton.
" John Liggett.
" David W. Moore.

* Minutes of Newcastle Pres.; Minutes of Pres. of Philadelphia; Cruise of the " Potomac;" Personal Reminiscences.

REV. ROBERT M'CACHRAN.

Robert M'Cachran, of Scotch-Irish ancestry, was born and grew to manhood almost within hearing of the weekly services of the sanctuary. Having become hopefully pious, and believing it to be his duty to enter the Christian ministry, he commenced the study of the classics at the Brandywine Academy, then under the direction of the Rev. John W. Grier.

After the retirement of Mr. Grier and the discontinuance of the Academy, Mr. M'Cachran finished his preparatory training at the Rev. Dr. M'Graw's Academy, in Cecil County, Md. His collegiate course was completed at Dickinson College, during the presidency of Dr. Mason, and his theological in the Seminary at Princeton, N. J.

He was licensed to preach the Gospel by the Presbytery of Newcastle in 1827, and having spent some time in supplying churches without a pastor, he accepted a call from the congregation of Big Spring, now Newville, Cumberland County, Pa., and was installed in the Spring of 1830. He remained in this connection until October, 1851, when a chronic affection of the chest compelled him to resign his charge.

After his withdrawal from the active duties of the ministry, Mr. M'Cachran resided in Newville, and devoted a portion of his time to the superintendence of a classical school. The congregation at Newville during his pastorate received many tokens of Divine favor. While he had charge nearly five hundred members were added to the church, seventy-three of them the fruits of a revival which occurred the second year of his ministry.

Mr. M'Cachran resided at Newville without a charge until his death, February 15, 1885, having been for some years the oldest member of the Presbytery of Carlisle, with which he had been connected upwards of half a century. He was the first member of the congregation who entered the ministry during the pastorate of Dr. Grier.*

REV. ANDERSON B. QUAY.

Anderson B. Quay, a native of Chester County, Pa., was born in 1802. He had married and was engaged in business when a change in his religious views led him to consider it his duty to preach the Gospel. He, therefore, after due preparation in the Academy at Reading, Pa., entered the Seminary at Princeton in 1827, where he remained until September, 1829.

Mr. Quay was licensed by the Presbytery of Newcastle, October 7, 1829. On the 6th of April, 1830, he was dismissed to the Presbytery of Carlisle, and passed the next two years as a probationer, supplying the united congregations of Monaghan, now Dillsburg, and Petersburg, both in York County, Pa. In the Spring of 1832 he was installed pastor of those Churches by the Presbytery of Carlisle. His labors among the people of his charge continued with in-

---

* Dr. Nevin, "Churches of the Valley;" Com. from James M'Cachran; Minutes of Presbytery of Carlisle; Local Memoranda.

creasing benefit until the Autumn of 1839, when the pastoral relation was dissolved at his request, and he accepted an Agency from the Presbyterian Board of Education.

In May, 1840, he became pastor of the First Presbyterian Church at Beaver, Pa., continuing to act a part of the time as Agent of the Board. His pastorate at Beaver lasted until February, 1842, when he received an appointment from the Board of Foreign Missions and resigned his charge. The members of the congregation parted with much regret from the pastor whose services, owing to their pecuniary circumstances, they were unable properly to recompense.

Mr. Quay held the position of Agent of the Board of Missions about a year, when he accepted a call to Indiana, Pa., where he remained until 1849. In the last-named year, at the request of the Colonization Society of Pennsylvania, he became their Agent, and retained the position until his death, which took place at Beaver in 1856.

Mr. Quay united with pleasing manners great firmness of purpose and warmth of feeling. He faithfully discharged the duties of pastor to the congregations intrusted to his oversight, and labored diligently for the promotion of Education, Foreign Missions, and African Colonization. His eldest son, Matthew Stanley Quay, was recently the able and popular Secretary of the Commonwealth.*

---

* Min. of Pres. of Newcastle; Min. of Pres. of Carlisle; Rev. J. J. Scatterfield, " Hist. of First Pres. Church of Beaver."

REV. BRITTON E. COLLINS.

Britton Estol Collins was born in Philadelphia, February 2, 1802. Having settled within the bounds of this congregation, he was brought to a knowledge of Jesus Christ as the only Saviour, and led to devote himself to the ministry of Reconciliation by the preaching of the Rev. Dr. J. N. C. Grier.

Mr. Collins pursued his classical studies under the direction of the Rev. John W. Grier, and in the Fall of 1824 entered the Seminary at Princeton, where he remained two years. He was licensed by the Presbytery of Philadelphia in April, 1828, and passed the next two years preaching as a probationer.

On the 7th of April, 1830, Mr. Collins was received as a licentiate by the Presbytery of Huntingdon, and in June (16th) of the same year was ordained as an Evangelist. He received a call from the church at Millerstown, Perry County, Pa., April 4, 1832, and was installed in October of that year.

Mr. Collins resigned his charge at Millerstown April 9, 1839, and the next October received a call to Shirleysburg, which he declined, but consented to act as a stated supply. He remained at Shirleysburg until October, 1853, when he retired, but continued to labor as a missionary within the bounds of the Presbytery of Huntingdon until the infirmities of age unfitted him for the active duties of the ministry. At his death, which took place at Shirleysburg, April 12, 1876, he was the oldest member of that Presbytery.

A faithful servant of the Master, after a life of usefulness, with the petition on his lips, "Thy will be done," he entered into rest.*

REV. BENJAMIN M. NYCE.

Benjamin M. Nyce was born near Pughtown, Chester County. While he was still a minor his father, John Nyce, removed and settled near Wagontown, within the bounds of Dr. Grier's charge. Having become connected with the congregation worshipping in this place, Mr. Nyce was finally led to consider it his duty to make known the glad tidings of salvation. He passed some time in the study of the classics in the Brandywine Academy, then under the direction of the Rev. John W. Grier, and entered Dickinson College, where he was graduated in September, 1829.

He taught the next three years in the Deaf and Dumb Asylum, Philadelphia, and in the Autumn of 1833 entered the Seminary at Princeton, where he remained one year. But of his subsequent history the writer after diligent inquiry has been unable to obtain any reliable information. The probability is that he died shortly after completing his preparation for the ministry.†

---

* "Hist. of Presbytery of Huntingdon;" Necrology of Princeton Seminary; *Presbyterian Banner*.

† Records of Princeton Seminary; Records of Deaf and Dumb Asylum; "Reminiscences of Rev. R. M'Cachran."

REV. RICHARD WALKER.

Richard, eldest son of Richard and Sarah (Henderson) Walker, was born at Indian Town, Wallace Township, May 1, 1812. He was engaged for some years in mechanical pursuits, but finally relinquished them to enter the Gospel ministry. After due preparation he was licensed by the New School Presbytery of Philadelphia, and supplied for a time the church at Womelsdorf, Berks County.

In April, 1842, he was sent as a supply to the Presbyterian Church at Allentown, Lehigh County, Pa. His ministry there was so successful that in May, 1844, he was installed as pastor of the congregation worshipping in that church. He remained in charge until 1859, when bodily infirmity compelled him to withdraw from continuous ministerial labor.

He subsequently preached in different places when his health permitted until a short time before his death, which occurred at Allentown on the 10th of May, 1882.

Mr. Walker was unassuming, earnest, and sincere, and the members of his charge parted with regret from the pastor whose unremitted endeavors to promote their spiritual interests had rendered him incapable of any but partial labor in the Gospel field.*

---

* Necrology of Princeton Seminary; Obituary Notice, *Graphic*; Com. from Samuel Walker.

REV. REES HAPPERSETT, D.D.

Dr. Happersett, the youngest son of Melchi and Rebecca (Graham) Happersett, was born in West Nantmeal Township, Chester County, July 31, 1810. He became the subject of Divine Grace during the great revival of 1831 in Dr. Grier's congregation, of which his parents had long been members. His academical studies were prosecuted at New London in this County, and his collegiate at Washington College, Pa., where he was graduated in 1836. He completed his theological course in the Seminary at Princeton, N. J., three years afterwards, and was licensed by the Presbytery of Newcastle in September, 1839.

Shortly after his licensure, Dr. Happersett became pastor of the Presbyterian Church at Havre de Grace, Md., where he remained about a year. He then entered the service of the Board of Domestic Missions, and for upwards of twenty years was diligently engaged in increasing its means and usefulness.

While he was connected with that Board, Dr. Happersett visited and preached in many of the Southern States. He also supplied, at different times, the vacant pulpits of several churches in Pennsylvania, among others the church at Waynesburg (Honeybrook) upwards of six months.

Having observed, during his visits to California, the scarcity of laborers in the Gospel field of that State, he determined to aid the efforts which were making to unfurl and uphold the banner of Presbyterianism in the settlements on the "Pacific Slope." He, therefore, resigned his office in the Board of Missions in the Fall of 1861, proceeded immediately to San Francisco, and passed the next six months preaching in that city and vicinity.

In the Spring of 1862 he accepted a unanimous call to the pastorate of the First Presbyterian Church at Stockton, Cal., where he ministered with increasing acceptance and benefit until his death, in September, 1866.

The degree of D.D. was conferred on him by Jefferson College in 1856.*

REV. JUSTUS UMSTEAD.

Rev. Justus Umstead, whose parents were members of Dr. Grier's congregation, is a graduate of the University of Pennsylvania, and of the Theological Seminary at Princeton, New Jersey.

He was licensed by the Presbytery of Philadelphia in July, 1847, and settled shortly after at South Bend, Ind., where he remained about a year. He then became pastor of the Presbyterian Church at Muscatine, Iowa, and after a successful ministry of three years removed to Keokuk in the same State. Mr. Umstead remained at Keokuk, in the faithful discharge of his pastoral duties, until the Fall of 1860, when he

---

* Com. from the late Mrs. Agnes Happersett; Minutes of Pres. of Newcastle; Minutes of Board of Domestic Missions.

accepted a call from the church at Fagg's Manor, Pa., where he was installed in November, 1860.

His labors at Fagg's Manor were not without encouragement. In 1865 there was an awakening, by which one hundred and fifty-seven "were added to the Lord."

In May, 1872, the pastoral relation was dissolved, and he took charge of the Presbyterian Church at St. George's, Delaware. He remained until 1876, when he resigned and became pastor of the church at Smyrna in the same State, where he is still engaged in ministerial work with marked success.*

REV. JAMES G. RALSTON, D.D., LL.D.

Dr. Ralston, widely known as a successful educator, and a minister of the Gospel, was born in Wallace Township, Chester County. He united at an early age with the congregation worshipping in this place, and directed his attention to a preparation for the ministry of the New Testament. His academical training was obtained at New London and Hopewell Academies in this County, and his collegiate at Washington College, Pennsylvania, where he was graduated September 26, 1838.

He taught the next two years after his graduation in an academy at Steubenville, Ohio, pursuing at the same time the study of Theology under the direction of the principal of the academy, the Rev. John W.

---

* Rev. W. B. Noble, "History of Fagg's Manor;" MSS.

Scott, D.D. In June, 1840, he entered the Theological Seminary at Princeton, New Jersey, where he completed his studies for the ministry.

Dr. Ralston was licensed by the Presbytery of Newcastle, April 14, 1841, and accepted a mission to the Winnebago Indians. But his health failing before he reached his destination, he was obliged reluctantly to abandon the undertaking. His health having been in a measure restored, he preached for some months as a supply to the Church at Florence, in the bounds of the Presbytery of Washington.

In October, 1841, Dr. Ralston entered on what proved to be the main business of his life, as principal of the Female Seminary at Oxford, Chester County, Pa. He remained at Oxford until the close of October, 1845, when he opened the now well-known Oakland Female Institute at Norristown, Montgomery County, Pa. There his industry, ability, and faithfulness as an instructor soon resulted in a large and annually increasing patronage. The upwards of twenty-five hundred ladies who have been educated wholly or in part in that institution have exerted and are exerting an influence whose usefulness can never be fully estimated. At the fireside, in the school-room, and the church, and among the benighted of heathen lands, the results of their judicious mental and religious training must be traced.

In addition to the discharge of his onerous duties as principal of a large educational institution, Dr. Ralston frequently supplied the pulpits of churches without a pastor, and assisted his clerical brethren during revivals and on other occasions. He was also during the last seventeen years of his life an efficient member of the Board of Publication of the Presbyterian Church.

The degree of LL.D. was conferred on him by Lafayette College, Easton, Pa., in 1865, and of D.D. by his Alma Mater two years afterwards.

Dr. Ralston died November 10, 1880, in the sixty-fifth year of his age.*

REV. WILLIAM PINKERTON.

William Pinkerton, an elder brother of the Rev. John Pinkerton, was born in October, 1809. Having been hopefully converted during the great refreshing from on High in 1831, he resolved to dedicate himself to the work of the Gospel ministry.

His preparatory studies were pursued at New London Academy, Chester County, and his collegiate at Washington College, Pennsylvania, where he was graduated in September, 1836. His theological course was completed at Princeton in 1839. On the 10th of the next September he was licensed by the Presbytery of Newcastle, and settled shortly afterwards as Pastor of the Cove Church, Albemarle County, Va. He also ministered to the High Bridge Church, Rockbridge County, Va., and to Collierstown Church in the same county.

During the last sixteen years of his life he had

---

* Futhey, "Hist. of Chester County;" Com. from John K. Ralston.

the pastoral oversight of Mount Carmel Church, Augusta County, Va.

Mr. Pinkerton was a diligent worker in the Master's vineyard. Uniting a ready command of language with fervid piety, his services in the Sanctuary were largely attended and blessed by the conversion of many.

Besides the faithful discharge of his duties to the congregations committed to his care, he established and conducted a classical school, and also successfully labored in the revival of churches which had either grown feeble or been partially abandoned. Among these was Mountain Plain, where, more than a hundred years before, Mr. Black, the first pastor of Brandywine Manor Church, had spent the last years of his ministry.

Mr. Pinkerton died March 13, 1875.*

REV. WILLIAM H. TEMPLETON.

William H. Templeton, eldest son of John Templeton, Esq., who was upwards of thirty years a Ruling Elder of this church, commenced his academical studies at New London, Chester County, in 1841. He entered Washington College, Pennsylvania, in November, 1843, and was graduated in 1845. He passed the next two years teaching, and then became a member of the

---

* Futhey, "History of Upper Oct. Church;" Com. from Frank D. Pinkerton; MSS.

seminary at Princeton, New Jersey, where his theological course was completed.

Mr. Templeton was licensed by the Presbytery of New Brunswick in September, 1850, and the next October went as a missionary to the Creek Indians, Indian Territory. He remained in that Territory until 1857, when the death of his wife and his impaired health caused him to return to Pennsylvania.

Being unable to endure the labor to which he had been subjected, Mr. Templeton withdrew from the missionary field; but in 1858 settled in Illinois, where he is still engaged in ministerial labor.*

REV. JOHN PINKERTON.

John Pinkerton, third son of John W. and Agnes Pinkerton, was born near Sadsburyville, Chester County, Pa., in November, 1811. When he was about six years of age his parents, who were members of the Upper Octoraro Presbyterian Church, removed to Honeybrook Township, and connected themselves with the congregation worshipping in this place.

Mr. Pinkerton passed his early years, like many young men, without any serious thoughts on the subject of religion until 1831, when he was awakened to a sense of his lost condition during the remarkable revival which commenced in that year. His convictions were deep and pungent, and he was so weighed down by the burden of sin that his health became

---

* Minutes of Presbytery of New Brunswick; Com. from the late J. G. Templeton; MS. Collections.

impaired. But obeying the Saviour's command, "Come unto me all ye that are weary and heavy laden," he found pardon and peace.

Having determined to obtain a classical education, Mr. Pinkerton entered the Academy at Lewisburg, Union County, Pa., May 15, 1837. He completed his preparatory studies in it and the Academy at Mifflinburg in the same county at the close of 1841, and was graduated at the College of New Jersey in 1843. After the usual Theological Course at Princeton, he taught some time in a classical school which his brother, the Rev. William Pinkerton, had established.

The Presbytery of Greenbrier licensed him to preach the Gospel in October, 1849. He assisted the Rev. Samuel R. Houston, of Monroe County, Va., in teaching and ministerial labor until October, 1853, when he accepted a call from the congregation of Mossy Creek Presbyterian Church, Augusta County, Va. Mr. Pinkerton was ordained and installed November 5, 1853, and this relation continued until his death, May 31, 1871, left the people of his charge to mourn the loss of their zealous, beloved, and faithful pastor.

The possessor of abilities and acquirements which would have enabled him to attain eminence in almost any department of literature, Mr. Pinkerton devoted the talents committed to his care to the service of his Divine Master, and instead of earthly honors, chose rather to be an humble disciple of Him "who went about doing good."*

---

* Memorial by Rev. William T. Price; Records of Lewisburg Academy; Personal Reminiscences.

COATESVILLE PRESBYTERIAN CHURCH.

COATESVILLE, though settled at an early period, remained without a house for public worship until 1831. In that year the members of Baptist, Episcopal, Friends', Methodist, and Presbyterian Churches residing in and near the village, with a Christian harmony worthy of record, uniting their efforts and means, built a meeting-house.

Among those who occupied its pulpit, on the part of the Presbyterians, when his other duties permitted, was the Rev. A. G. Morrisson, pastor of the congregations of Doe Run and Union. His services were so acceptable, and the number of his hearers increased so much, that in 1833 a petition was presented to Presbytery for the organization of a Church at Coatesville. The request was not granted, but being renewed at the next meeting of Presbytery, it was favorably received and a Committee appointed, which met in September (4th), 1833, and organized the Presbyterian Church of Coatesville.

The congregation, which had been gathered principally by the care and faithfulness of Mr. Morrisson, in March of the next year presented a call for one-half of his time. This he accepted, and having obtained a release from the pastorate of the Union Church, was installed on the 24th of April, 1834.

Under his ministry the number of members became

so large that they found it necessary to have a meeting-house of their own. They therefore obtained the interest in the building and lot of those who had contributed funds for the purpose.*

Having increased facilities for public worship, the congregation became sufficiently numerous to sustain weekly services in the sanctuary, and a call was accordingly presented to Presbytery on the 14th of April, 1857, for the whole of Mr. Morrisson's time. The request was granted, his relation at Doe Run dissolved, and he devoted the whole of his labor to the church at Coatesville.

How faithfully he performed the duties of an "ambassador for Christ" is shown by the increasing membership of the church, the flourishing condition of its Sunday-School, its liberal contributions for benevolent purposes, and the warm affection which existed between the pastor and his people.

But "the prophets do not live forever," and, in 1868, the infirmities of nearly threescore and ten caused Mr. Morrisson to offer his resignation. The members of his flock, however, could not endure the thought of parting with the pastor who had been connected with the church from its beginning, and who, for a third of a century, had been to many of them a guide and counsellor, a "more than friend." They therefore generously resolved to provide a colleague and to continue to pay Mr. Morrisson a portion of his salary during his life.

---

* They occupied this building until 1849, when it was replaced by a new church edifice, and this, in 1867, was enlarged to its present size.

In accordance with this resolution, the congregation gave a call in January (15th), 1868, to the present pastor, the Rev. James Roberts, who was ordained and installed May 28, 1868. The relation thus established between the aged servant of God and his younger brother continued "harmoniously and pleasantly" until the death of Mr. Morrisson, October 27, 1870.

Dr. Roberts, who is a native of Montrose, Scotland, received his classical education at Media, Delaware County, Pa., where he passed some time as an instructor. He was graduated at Lafayette College, Easton, Pa., in July, 1865, and at the Theological Seminary, Princeton, N. J., a few weeks before his installation at Coatesville.

During his pastorate the membership of the church, now upwards of three hundred, has annually increased. The Sunday-School, which was conducted many years by the same Superintendent, continues to flourish, and in numbers, influence, and liberality the Presbyterians, under the guidance of Dr. Roberts, are the leading denomination in that borough.

Dr. Roberts, who is equally and deservedly esteemed by his clerical brethren and the people of his charge, was sent as a Commissioner to the General Assembly in 1872, and also in 1877. Since April, 1869, he has been the stated clerk of Presbytery, and in 1883 received the honorary degree of D.D. from Lafayette College, Pennsylvania.

A centre of manufacturing industry, and situated on one of the great thoroughfares of trade, Coatesville must necessarily increase in wealth and population.

But from the nature of their occupations many of its inhabitants will be only transient residents. Withdrawn from the kindly influence of home, exposed to numerous temptations, and often suddenly deprived of employment by the vicissitudes of business, they, above most others, will always need the restraining, consoling, and saving influence of the Gospel. It is, therefore, a cause for thankfulness that, in Coatesville, the opportunities to hear the words of truth have kept pace with the growth of the population. Where, in 1830, there was not a single building set apart for public worship, the voice of prayer, admonition, and praise may now be heard, on every returning Sabbath, in six meeting-houses dedicated to the service of the Triune God.*

---

* Minutes of Presbytery of Newcastle; Dr. Roberts, "Pastoral of Coatesville Pres. Church."

HONEYBROOK PRESBYTERIAN CHURCH.

When Dr. Grier's congregation had become so large that it was necessary for a portion to withdraw, those residing near the western boundary of his charge obtained a site in the village of Honeybrook, erected a house for public worship, and having received permission from the Presbytery, were organized as the Honeybrook Presbyterian Church, November 28, 1835.

They were dependent on supplies until May, 1837, when the Rev. William W. Latta, who had been given a unanimous call to become their pastor, was ordained and installed. Mr. Latta remained, with increasing popularity and usefulness, until the Fall of 1858, when failing health caused him to obtain a release from his charge.

Unassuming, kind, and faithful, Mr. Latta was much beloved by the members of the congregation, and they parted with regret from the pastor under whose guidance many of them had found "joy and peace in believing."

Mr. Latta was succeeded by the Rev. John G. Thom, who was installed May 19, 1859. Mr. Thom, like the Apostle to the Gentiles, "was in labors abundant." Besides the services of the sanctuary, he preached and conducted weekly prayer-meetings in different parts of his charge, and was active in the furtherance of Sunday-Schools and temperance. He also aided his fellow-citizens by his counsel and example during the struggle to maintain the Union.

Having declined several invitations to take the oversight of congregations without a pastor, Mr. Thom at last accepted a call to St. Louis, Mo., and was installed in October, 1865. But he had scarcely entered on his field of labor when, enfeebled by his previous discharge of pastoral duties, he sunk under an attack of typhoid fever and entered into rest.

The successor of Mr. Thom was the Rev. J. H. Young, who became pastor in 1866, and remained until March 7, 1869, when the pastoral relation was dissolved by the Presbytery of Donegal.

Mr. Young is a ready speaker, a sound theologian, and a good classical scholar. He is now professor of Languages in the Normal School in Indiana, Pa.

The congregation next presented a unanimous call to the Rev. William Ferguson, of Dubuque, Iowa, which he accepted, and was installed in October, 1869.

In the Fall of 1871, Mr. Ferguson was released at his own request by the Presbytery of Chester. The ministry of Mr. Ferguson was not without its fruits, eighty-six having been added to the church while he had charge.

He is now pastor of the Presbyterian Church at Pittsgrove, N. J., where his labors have met with encouraging success.

In June, 1872, the congregation gave a unanimous call to the Rev. William W. Totheroth, who was installed by a Committee of the Presbytery of Chester on the last day of October, 1872. In 1883, Mr.

Totheroth received and accepted a call to become pastor of a Church at Le Roy, N. Y.

The pastorate of Mr. Totheroth was eminently beneficial. His zeal, prudence, and industry promoted harmony, increased the membership of the church, and imparted renewed activity to its benevolent operations.

In the amount of its donations for charitable purposes, the number of its members, and of children attending its Sabbath-Schools, this church ranks among the first of the rural Presbyterian Churches in our State. It has contributed to the growth of the village in which its meeting-house is placed, and, like orthodox churches in general, is a nucleus around which enterprise, refinement, and intelligence have clustered.*

---

* Minutes of Presbytery of Donegal; Rev. Mr. Totheroth, "Hist. of Church;" Local Memoranda.

FAIRVIEW PRESBYTERIAN CHURCH.

On account of the distance which they had to travel in order to attend the services of the sanctuary, and for other reasons which need not be stated, the members of Dr. Grier's congregation who resided in the northeastern part of his charge resolved to erect a building for public worship and obtain a distinct organization. Accordingly, having procured an elevated and beautiful site, easy of access, and convenient, they commenced in 1839 the erection of a meeting-house, which was completed and dedicated on the first day of the next year.

In May, 1840, a Committee of the Third Presbytery of Philadelphia met and organized a church under the name of the West Nantmeal Presbyterian Church.*

The same month (May, 1840) the Rev. Alexander Porter, who had received his classical and theological education in the College and Seminary at Princeton, N. J., was ordained and installed as pastor. Mr. Porter was released from his charge in May, 1843. During his pastorate forty-three were added to the membership of the church.

Mr. Porter was succeeded, in October, 1843, by the Rev. William H. McCarter, a graduate of Jefferson

---

* The name of the Township in which it is situated having been changed, it is now called Fairview Presbyterian Church.

College, Pennsylvania, and of Union Theological Seminary, New York. Mr. McCarter labored with fidelity and acceptance until October, 1849, when he received a call to the pastoral oversight of a Presbyterian Church at Edwardsville, Indiana, and removed to that State.

The successor of Mr. McCarter was the Rev. B. B. Hotchkin, late pastor of Marple Presbyterian Church, Delaware County. While Dr. Hotchkin, who is well known as an author and an earnest, impressive speaker, had charge the church was highly prosperous. In June, 1859, Dr. Hotchkin, always desirous of enlarging his sphere of usefulness, accepted a call to his late pastorate, where his ministrations were greatly blessed.*

The next year the church was dependent on supplies, but in October, 1860, the Rev. D. C. Meeker became pastor. Mr. Meeker, who received his collegiate training in the University of New York, and his theological at Union Seminary in New York State, remained until October, 1868, when he was called to labor in another part of the Master's vineyard. His relations with the members of his flock were harmonious and pleasant, and they parted with regret from their faithful shepherd.

After the retirement of Mr. Meeker, the congregation obtained the services of the Rev. A. Nelson Hollifield, who discharged his pastoral duties with much ability until the close of 1875, when he accepted a unanimous call to the Presbyterian Church of Huntingdon, Pa., where he was installed in January, 1876.

---

* Dr. Hotchkin died October 13, 1878, in the seventy-second year of his age.

During his ministry one hundred and thirty-three were added to the membership of the church, and the meeting-house, which had become much impaired, was replaced by a large and commodious structure, at a cost of thirteen thousand dollars.

In May, 1876, the Rev. William Boyd, who was graduated with honor at the University of Pennsylvania, and completed his theological course in the Seminary at Princeton, was installed. Young, ardent, and gifted, Mr. Boyd soon won the confidence of the community, and his field of usefulness rapidly increased.*

Besides a well-attended Sunday-School, conducted in the church building, another is maintained during the summer season in an outlying portion of the congregation, a short distance from Loag's Corner, where there is also stated preaching every month.

Surrounded by a rural but thrifty and intelligent population, with a new church edifice, a parsonage, and a beautiful cemetery, all without incumbrance, Fairview Church cannot fail to increase in numbers and usefulness, nor cease to diffuse the blessings of order, temperance, and piety.†

---

* In March, 1883, Mr. Boyd, much to the regret of his congregation, received and accepted a call to become pastor of the Second Presbyterian Church of Camden, N. J. He was succeeded in September of the same year by the Rev. William P. Breed, Jr., a son of the Rev. Dr. Breed of the West Spruce Street Church, Philadelphia.

† "History of Fairview Church," by Rev. W. Boyd; Local Memoranda.

CENTRAL PRESBYTERIAN CHURCH, DOWNINGTOWN, PA.

Downingtown, one of the oldest towns in Chester County, was settled by members of the Society of Friends who had emigrated from Wales. The site was well chosen, being near to the "Indian Trail" leading from the Delaware to the Susquehanna, and in the midst of a beautiful and fertile valley. Besides, it was supplied by one of the main branches of the Brandywine with abundance of water-power, so important in a new settlement.

Possessing these advantages, it might have been supposed that the growth of Downingtown would be rapid, and that, like Lancaster, Reading, and other inland towns, it would, ere long, rise to the dignity of a city. But its inhabitants, satisfied with their possessions and pursuits, not only advanced slowly in the march of improvement, but even rejected proffered sources of wealth and importance; among others a proposition to make their village the seat of justice when Chester County was divided.

There was consequently little opportunity or inducement for the active and enterprising Scotch and Scotch-Irish to make it their home and establish the church of their fathers. It should, therefore, not excite surprise that near a century and a half passed after the first settlement of Downingtown before a Presbyterian Church was organized within its limits.

In 1843 some God-fearing men, whom the activity and business introduced by the Pennsylvania Railroad, and the spirit of enterprise in general, had caused to settle at Downingtown, adopted measures leading to the establishment of a Presbyterian Church. Neighboring clergymen of that denomination were invited to preach, and religious services were held at private residences and in school-houses and halls obtained for the purpose. Their number increased slowly, but in 1860 they felt sufficiently encouraged to undertake the building of a church edifice. Accordingly, they obtained a lot and erected a meeting-house.

Owing, however, to causes which it would be neither beneficial nor perhaps possible to trace, dissensions arose, many withdrew from the church, pecuniary difficulties increased, and the building was finally sold and occupied for secular purposes.

But the Christian men and women who were attached to the doctrines and government of the Presbyterian Church did not despair. Believing that the Most High would cause light to shine out of darkness, they faithfully and prayerfully continued the good work, and in October, 1861, had the satisfaction of seeing the Central Presbyterian Church of Downingtown organized by a Committee of the Presbytery of Newcastle.

The congregation was dependent for some time on supplies, but in 1862 extended a call to the Rev. Matthew Newkirk, who was ordained and installed April 24, 1862.

Under his faithful oversight the membership of the church increased so much that it was determined to erect a house for public worship. The building was commenced in June, 1863, but, owing to unforeseen causes of delay, it was not completed and dedicated until August, 1864.

Mr. Newkirk, who considered no labor too humble or too severe provided it furthered the interests of his people, remained until 1868, when he became pastor of a church in Philadelphia.[*]

Mr. Newkirk was succeeded by the Rev. John Rae, a licentiate of the Western Theological Seminary, at Alleghany, Pa. Mr. Rae continued in charge until April, 1872, when he obtained his release and went as a missionary to Washington Territory.

The pastorate of Mr. Rae, though short, was not without its beneficial results. While he occupied the pulpit fifty united with the church, several of them in the morning of life.

The present pastor, the Rev. Francis J. Collier, a graduate of Jefferson College, Cannonsburg, Pa., and of the Theological Seminary at Princeton, succeeded Mr. Rae, and was installed October 7, 1872.

Mr. Collier is a ready speaker, and his expositions of Divine truth are well calculated to arouse the conscience and impress the heart. Since his connection with the church its membership has continually increased. Seasons of awakening have occurred, in

---

[*] Mr. Newkirk has recently resigned the pastorate of Bethlehem Presbyterian Church, corner of Broad and Diamond Streets, Philadelphia.

which many "have been born again." The well-conducted Sunday-School is becoming more and more efficient, and both the pastor and his people are earnestly engaged in extending the blessed influence of the Gospel of Him at whose advent was proclaimed peace on earth and good will to men.*

* "History of the Church," by the present pastor; Minutes of Presbytery; Local Memoranda.

ACADEMIES.

BRANDYWINE ACADEMY.

A SCHOOL was opened for instruction in the classics and the higher branches of science about 1792 in a part of the building, which stood until 1863, immediately West of the Upper Graveyard.

This school, which was a necessary adjunct to the Theological School, was placed at first under the direction of the Rev. Mr. McPherson, a native of Ireland, who was subsequently deposed from the ministry on account of intemperance and died in the Chester County poor-house.

After the withdrawal of Mr. McPherson, Mr. Matthew G. Wallace, a graduate of the College of New Jersey in 1795, became principal. He remained, pursuing at the same time his studies in theology under the direction of the Rev. Nathan Grier until his licensure, in 1799, when the school was closed.

In 1802 it was reopened by Mr. John Ralston, of Cumberland County, Pa., also a theological student. He died in the fall of 1804, and Dr. John F. Grier, who in the spring of that year had opened a classical school in Pequea, took charge of it. He discharged the duties of principal with much ability until his settlement at Reading, in 1809, when the school was suspended. It was subsequently conducted about three years by the Rev. John W. Grier, who resigned in March or April, 1822, and removed to the Chester County Academy. After the retirement of Mr. Grier the school was finally closed.

At this Academy, which was the first institution of a higher grade than a common school opened in this part of Chester County, the Rev. Drs. D. Elliott, J. F. Grier, J. N. C. Grier, and the Rev. Messrs. Hood, Kennedy, J. H. Grier, J. W. Grier, R. S. Grier, J. Buchanan, J. E. Grier, M.D., Matthew Grier, M.D., Benjamin Griflith, M.D., and the Hon. David Potts received the whole of their preparatory training in the classical languages and English Literature.

The Rev. Messrs. A. G. Morrison, Robert M'Cachran, and Benjamin M. Nyce also passed some time in studying the Greek and Roman Classics at this Institution.

So far as is known this Academy was well conducted, and its pupils exerted a wide-spread, beneficial influence.*

HOWARD ACADEMY.

This Institution was opened for the reception of pupils November 13, 1848, in the village of Rockville. It was under the direction of Elder John Ralston and his brother James, as proprietors, and a graduate of the College of New Jersey, who had

* "Reminiscences of Rev. Dr. Grier;" Com. from Rev. R. McCachran; MSS.

spent several years in teaching, as principal. At first this school was regarded by many as a doubtful experiment. But it soon became favorably known, and attracted pupils from every part, not only of Chester County, but also from the cities of Lancaster, Reading, and Philadelphia.

The instruction was thorough, and the course of study embraced all that is required for admission to our best colleges or for an entrance on the study of any of the learned professions.

With the exception of three months, when his place was supplied by the Rev. Mr. Ogden, of Easton, it continued with increasing patronage and usefulness under the superintendence of the first Principal, until September, 1855, when, having accepted a professorship in one of our large cities, he resigned.

After his withdrawal a select school was kept in the building by Miss Louisa Ralston, of Honeybrook. It was subsequently conducted as an academy by Mr. Watson, of Milton, Pa., who was succeeded by the Rev. Mr. Kirkland, a native of Scotland, noted for his superior classical attainments and his accurate acquaintance with history. But owing to the institution having been several times discontinued and to other causes which it is neither important nor perhaps possible to trace, its popularity declined, and in September, 1862, it was finally closed.*

In addition to upwards of thirty who have been successful as teachers and others who engaged with

---

* See Appendix L.

advantage in agricultural, mechanical, or mercantile pursuits, the following members of the learned professions received a part or the whole of their preparatory training in this Academy:

REV. JOHN C. THOMPSON.

Mr. Thompson was graduated at Lafayette College in 1855, completed his theological course at Princeton in 1858, and was licensed by the Presbytery of Newcastle in the Spring of the following year.

Shortly after his licensure he accepted an invitation to supply the First Presbyterian Church, Nashville, Tenn., and resided in that city until the Rebellion forced him to withdraw. He then settled as pastor of the Presbyterian Church at Smyrna, Del., but in 1864 took charge of the Presbyterian Church at Pottstown, Montgomery County, Pa. He remained there, earnestly and faithfully discharging the duties of his charge, until 1873, when he accepted a call from the Presbyterian Church at Hagerstown, Md. During his pastorate the church edifice was replaced by a beautiful and commodious structure, and his ministrations there as elsewhere were greatly blessed.

On the 1st of January, 1879, Mr. Thompson took charge of the Southwark Presbyterian Church, Philadelphia. In June, 1880, he was called to the South Broad Street Presbyterian Church, and in 1885, by a union of Broad Street Church with the Scotch Presbyterian Church, became pastor of the united church, which is rapidly increasing its membership and means of doing good.

REV. DAVID W. MOORE.

Mr. Moore received his diploma from the College of New Jersey in 1858, and was graduated at the Theological Seminary at that place in April, 1861. On the 5th of the succeeding May he was ordained and installed pastor of the Lower Brandywine Presbyterian Church, Delaware. While he had charge of that church Mr. Moore passed some months as a chaplain with the Army of the Potomac, then lying near Petersburg, Va. The pastoral relation was dissolved at his request in October, 1872, and he resided in the Southwestern States, chiefly in Mississippi, until October, 1873, when he accepted a unanimous call to become the pastor of the congregation at McVeytown, Mifflin County, Pa. In 1883 he resigned and became pastor of the Presbyterian Church at Kennett Square, Chester County, where he is laboring with great success.

Mr. Moore has always taken a warm interest in education, and his plain, practical discourses prove him to be an earnest and faithful disciple of his Divine Master.

REV. THOMAS M. GRIFFITH.

Mr. Griffith entered Dickinson College in the Autumn of 1854, and received the degree of A.B. four years later, standing the second in his class. He passed the next winter as a teacher at Chester, Pa., and in the Spring of 1859 was licensed to preach the Gospel by the Philadelphia Conference of the Methodist Episcopal Church.

Since his licensure Mr. Griffith has been engaged in the faithful discharge of the duties of his sacred office, with the exception of a part of one year, which he spent travelling through Europe, Egypt, and the Holy Land. He is one of the most popular pastors of the Methodist Episcopal Church, and is daily increasing his reputation and usefulness.

REV. JOHN A. LIGGETT, D.D.

Dr. John A. Liggett, a son of the late Elder Caleb Liggett, entered Lafayette College, Easton, in 1853, and was graduated in 1857. His theological studies were completed in the Seminary at Danville, Kentucky.

In 1861 he accepted a call to the Presbyterian Church at Crittenden, Ky., where he remained until 1864, when he became pastor of the Second Presbyterian Church of Rahway, N. J.

Since his connection with the church at Rahway there have been several outpourings of the Spirit among the people, and the membership of the church during his pastorate has been more than doubled.

Dr. Liggett's discourses in the pulpit exhibit a ready command of language, a familiar but not unpolished style, and an earnest desire to promote the everlasting welfare of his hearers.

The degree of D.D. was conferred on him at its last Commencement by Lafayette College.

REV. ISAAC MAST.

Mr. Mast was born near Morgantown, Berks County, Pa., October 14, 1835. After leaving the Academy, in September, 1855, he entered the Ohio Wesleyan University, where he was graduated in the Autumn of 1859. He taught the next winter at Reading, Pa., and joined the Philadelphia Conference of the Methodist Episcopal Church in 1860.

In 1871 his health failed and he passed a year in California. Having returned with renewed strength, he engaged, with his usual zeal and faithfulness, in ministerial work until the winter of 1875-76, when, being unable to continue his pulpit labors, he spent some months in Florida. But the balmy breezes of the Peninsula did not reinvigorate his physical system, and in June, 1876, he sank the victim of that widewasting disease, consumption.

While a student in the Academy, Mr. Mast was noted for the genial disposition, modesty, and earnest desire to do right, which endeared him in after-years both to his ministerial brethren and to the members of the congregations of which he had the pastoral oversight.

He published an account of his observations and adventures while sojourning in California. This work, entitled "The Gun, Rod, and Saddle," may be read with advantage by all who desire to increase their knowledge of the land of gold and romantic scenery.*

WILLIAM IRWIN, M.D.

Dr. Irwin studied medicine under the direction of Dr. Joseph Gaston, of Honeybrook (Waynesburg),

---

* MSS. Collections; Personal Reminiscences.

and received the degree of M.D. from Jefferson College in 1856. He married a daughter of the late John M. Mullin, Esq., of West Brandywine, in 1857, and settled the same year as a physician at Smyrna, Lancaster County, Pa. He remained at Smyrna with increasing patronage until 1865, when he removed to Christiana, on the southeastern boundary of the same County, where he soon obtained an extensive practice.

Dr. Irwin continued in the active discharge of his professional duties until his physical system, never robust, became so much impaired as to render him unable to satisfy the increasing demand for his services. Such, however, was his attachment to his calling, and his desire to assist those who needed medical aid, that he did not relinquish his attendance on his patients, when his health permitted, until a short period before his death. This took place on the 13th of November, 1877, in the fifty-first year of his age.

Dr. Irwin was a diligent student, who spared neither time nor money to make himself familiar with the requirements of his profession. He died much regretted by those who had shared his friendship and experienced the benefit of his medical skill.

H. CLAY MEREDITH, M.D.

Dr. Meredith completed his classical course at Oakland Institute and Poughkeepsie, N. Y. He pursued the study of medicine under the supervision of his father, the late Dr. Stephen Meredith, and was graduated at the Medical Department of the University of Pennsylvania in 1864. Immediately after his graduation Dr. Meredith entered the Army of the United

States as an assistant surgeon. He remained actively engaged until the close of the war, when he resigned and commenced the practice of his profession at Pughtown, Chester County.

Dr. Meredith, like his father, has the reputation of being a skilful, well-read physician, and his success justifies the confidence which is placed in his knowledge and ability.

JOHN WELLS, M.D.

Dr. Wells, after the close of his preparatory course at the Academy, entered the office of Dr. J. Rodebaugh, Charlestown Township, Chester County, as a student of medicine. He commenced his attendance on the lectures at the University of Pennsylvania in 1852, and received the degree of Doctor of Medicine from that institution in March, 1854.

Dr. Wells settled as a physician at his native place in Charlestown Township, and owing to his genial disposition and acknowledged ability was soon largely patronized. He continued the practice of his profession with increasing reputation and usefulness until his death, August 15, 1871.

The decease of Dr. Wells while still in the prime of life cast a gloom over a large circle of friends and acquaintances, who esteemed him as an upright citizen, and appreciated his worth as an attentive and skilful physician.

JOHN N. C. HAPPERSETT, M.D.

Dr. Happersett, a grandson of the Rev. Dr. J. N. C. Grier, read medicine with Dr. A. K. Gaston, of

West Brandywine Township, Chester County. He entered the Medical Department of Jefferson College in the Fall of 1857, and was graduated in March, 1859.

Dr. Happersett commenced the practice of his profession at Hollidaysburg, Pa., in the spring of 1860. His skill as a surgeon brought him into notice, and he was soon largely patronized.

On the outbreak of the Rebellion his patriotism led him to seek an appointment in the army. His application was successful, and in August, 1861, he was commissioned as an Assistant Surgeon. He served with distinction during the campaigns of the army of the West, and at the close of the war was assigned to the Department of the Carolinas. June 26, 1876, he was commissioned as "surgeon in full" and stationed at Fort Hamilton, in the Department of the East.

Dr. Happersett deservedly ranks high as a skilful surgeon and a successful practitioner, and the responsible position which he now holds in the army of the United States shows that he discharged the arduous duties of previous appointments with faithfulness and ability.

EUGENE GASTON, M.D.

Eugene, eldest son of the late Dr. A. K. Gaston, of West Brandywine, completed his classical education at the West Chester Academy. He read medicine under the direction of his father, entered the medical department of the University of Pennsylvania in

1863, and received the degree of M.D from that Institution in March, 1865.

Believing with Horace Greeley that the West affords the best opportunities for the employment of energy and ability, Dr. Gaston determined to become a resident of the Great Valley of the Mississippi, and settled as a practising physician in Vermilion County, Illinois, near the eastern boundary of that State. His success has justified the choice of his location, and the extensive and increasing demand for his services has exceeded the most sanguine expectations of both himself and his friends.

If length of days should be allotted him, Dr. Gaston, when near his threescore and ten, will no doubt merit and retain, as his father did, the patronage which he received during the preceding forty years.

ALFRED JONES, M.D.

When he withdrew from the Academy, where he had pursued his studies with diligence and success, Dr. Jones engaged in teaching a common school, but finally turned his attention to a preparation to enter the medical profession. Three years of close application were rewarded by the degree of M.D. from the University of Pennsylvania.

Immediately after his graduation he commenced the practice of medicine, which he pursued with encouraging success until the breaking out of the civil war, when his patriotism led him to enter the army. He received a commission as quartermaster from Governor Curtin, and accompanied the expedition to Beaufort, South Carolina. In July, 1864, he was taken prisoner while bearing despatches to General Hartranft, and did not obtain his release till near the close of hostilities, when he was mustered out of the service.

Before he resumed the practice of his profession Dr. Jones visited Europe, where he remained two years. While abroad he became a graduate of the Medical College of Paris, and attended the clinics of the hospitals of Vienna and Berlin. After his return he settled as a physician in Philadelphia, where his energy, perseverance, and faithful discharge of his professional duties have secured a large and lucrative practice.

Dr. Jones stands high in the estimation of the medical fraternity as a physician of skill, ability, and great moral worth.*

THOMAS BUCHANAN, M.D.

Thomas Buchanan, the younger son of the late Elder David Buchanan, of Honeybrook, passed three years at Millersville Normal School, Lancaster County, entered the freshman class of Amherst College, Mass., in 1864, and was graduated in 1868. He studied medicine under the direction of Prof. A. Pillou, of New York City, and attended the clinics in the hospitals of Paris, London, and St. Louis, Missouri.

Dr. Buchanan practised medicine several years, but on account of failing health relinquished his profession and became connected with the manufacturing interests of St. Louis, where he now resides. Like most

* MS. Collections.

patriotic young men, he passed 1861 to 1863 in the army.

Dr. Buchanan has diligently employed the advantages which he enjoyed, and is a learned and able physician. His withdrawal from the practice of his profession is a source of regret to his medical brethren and a loss to the community.*

DAVIS F. CROUSE, M.D.

Davis F. Crouse was born in Wallace, then a part of West Nantmeal Township, Chester County, April 29, 1835. His early instruction was received in the common schools, until the opening of Howard Academy, which he attended several sessions with marked diligence and improvement. In 1856 his parents removed to Illinois, where they had been settled but a short time when he commenced the study of medicine while teaching a public school. His studies were pursued with so much zeal and perseverance that three years afterwards he received the degree of M.D. from the Medical College at Cincinnati. In 1861–62 he attended the lectures of Bellevue Hospital, New York.

Dr. Crouse followed his profession with success in Carroll County, Ill., and subsequently in Joe Daviess County in the same State, but finally removed to Waterloo, Iowa, where he practised, in connection with a younger brother, until his retirement in 1878, after eighteen years of arduous professional labor. He then undertook the supervision of a nursery and a farm, in

---

* MS. Collections.

which he was engaged until his decease, in October, 1880.

Dr. Crouse's medical skill and attention to his patients caused him to be liberally patronized, while his amenity, upright conduct, and general culture gave him a high place in the estimation of both the public and his professional brethren.[*]

WILLIAM HUNTER, M.D.

William, only son of David Hunter, Esq., of Honeybrook Township, was born in July, 1833. Having completed his preparatory training at this Institution and the Academy at New London, he entered on the study of medicine under the direction of Dr. Atlee, of Lancaster, and received the degree of M.D. from the University of Pennsylvania in March, 1854.

Dr. Hunter settled as a physician at White Haven, Luzerne County, Pa., and pursued his profession with encouraging success and marked ability until the Spring of 1856, when he sunk under a chronic disease of the alimentary organs. His early death was the cause of much sorrow, not only to his bereaved sisters, but also to the many friends whose seemingly well-founded hopes of his professional eminence and usefulness, were unexpectedly blasted.

Dr. Hunter was the first of the students of Howard Academy who passed from the activity of professional life to the rest of the grave. His death, and the decease in less than thirty years of more than one-third

---

* MS. Collections.

of those who were pupils of the Institution, are melancholy proofs that youth is no protection against the shafts of the destroyer.

Howard Academy to a large number afforded the means of obtaining a better education than otherwise they could have done, and its discontinuance was a source of regret to the friends of intelligence and culture in Honeybrook and the neighboring Townships.

Besides weekly lectures by the principal on historical, literary, and scientific subjects, addresses to the students were delivered by the Rev. Drs. J. N. C. Grier, Lehman, Crowell, and Hotchkin, and the Rev. Messrs. W. W. Latta, Harry, Holland, Flowers, J. C. Thompson, and Dr. A. K. Gaston.*

---

* Reminiscences of First Principal; Records of Academy; Coms. from Elder John Ralston and others.

SUNDAY-SCHOOLS.

ROCKVILLE SUNDAY-SCHOOL.

In May, 1820, the first Sunday-School within the bounds of this congregation was organized in a building that stands a short distance north of Rockville, and which was long known by the name of Walker's School-House. Elder James Ralston, Elder William Templeton, Thomas M'Clune, and Obadiah Robinson were chosen Superintendents. As the first three were Presbyterians and the last named a Methodist, it was not strictly denominational, but was what would now be called a Union Sunday-School.

Elder John Ralston and his brother James, Jno. Dorlan, James Lockhart, Washington Righter, John Lockhart, Jos. Donnell, Master John W. Pinkerton, and perhaps some others, were selected as teachers. Master Pinkerton acted as Secretary.

Two of the Superintendents attended every Sabbath. One of them opened the School with prayer, and the other closed it in the same manner. The exercises consisted principally of the recitation of portions of the Scriptures and of Psalms and Hymns. There was a generous rivalry among the scholars in regard to the number of verses which each could recite on a Sabbath, and this emulation was carried so far that upwards of three hundred verses of the Bible were repeated by some of the pupils at one time.

The School assembled in the afternoon, and as it was somewhat of a novelty, the attendance was large, the children being accompanied in most instances by their parents.

The School building often proving too small to accommodate the scholars and spectators, the exercises were not unfrequently conducted in a grove which stood West of the road leading from the School-house to Rockville.

Dr. Grier, the pastor, occasionally attended, and gave the scholars some religious instruction and advice; but as he generally preached on the afternoon of the Sabbath, either in a school-house or at the residence of some aged member of the congregation, his engagements seldom permitted him to be present.

Tickets or cards with a text of Scripture printed on them were given to the scholars. Some of these tickets were printed on red paper, and others on blue. The recitation of a hymn, or of a fixed number of verses of Scripture, entitled a scholar to a blue card, and a certain amount of these could be exchanged for a red one. When the fortunate holder had obtained as many of the latter as were required, a book was given in their stead.

As the School had to be closed in the Fall, the discontinuance proved unfavorable, and when it was opened the next Spring the attendance was smaller, and the interest manifested much less. This became so apparent towards the end of the Summer, that those who were mainly instrumental in carrying it on were disheartened, and no arrangements were made for conducting it the next year.

In 1828 the School was reopened with but partial success. After that no effort was made to revive it until 1832, when it was reorganized by Elder William Templeton, who continued to be its efficient and faithful Superintendent until his death, in 1849. Ever since that time the School has been regularly kept open during the Summer season. Messrs. Thomas Walker, William Robinson, John F. Templeton, and Lewis Worrell have acted as Superintendents.

MANOR SUNDAY-SCHOOL.

A Sunday-School was opened in 1821 in the School building which stood near the Upper Graveyard. John Templeton, Esq., James K. Grier, Joseph F. Grier, M.D., John McCathran, James McCathran, William Major, William Stanly, and some others performed the duties of teachers. James Hindman filled the office of Secretary. The Rev. John W. Grier, who was at that time the Principal of the Brandywine Academy, acted as Superintendent. This School was in operation about two years, when it was discontinued.

In the Spring of 1828 a number of young people of the neighborhood met at the residence of General Matthew Stanly and organized a Sunday-School, which was held in a large spring-house loft belonging to the General. This School was mainly conducted by the same teachers as the one which had been kept in the school-house. It was continued during the

Summer season of two years, 1828 and 1829, when, owing to the unsafe condition of the walls of the building, it was thought imprudent to reopen it in the same place, and no other suitable building could be obtained.

After the lapse of several years a Sunday-School was opened in the Manor Church, under the superintendence of the Pastor, Dr. Grier. It was held in the morning, before the customary services of the day were commenced. Dr. Grier occupied a part of the time in explaining portions of the Scriptures and other religious exercises. This School, which was continued during the remainder of his pastorate, has been watched over and aided by his successors in the ministry. It has at present 112 scholars and 15 teachers and officers, with Mr. B. G. Rea as Superintendent.

Both it and the school at Rockville, which has 85 scholars and 11 teachers and officers, are regarded not only as important auxiliaries to the Church, but as a means of benefiting many who otherwise would receive no religious instruction.

The superintendents, all of the teachers, and many of the scholars connected with those first Sunday-Schools have passed away, while the survivors, with few exceptions, have numbered the allotted threescore and ten. But in reviewing the incidents of seventy years, there are scarcely any which they recall with more pleasure and gratitude than the associations and instruction of the weekly gatherings on the Sabbath which they attended more than half a century ago.

How many those primitive Sunday-Schools led

to become partakers of the blessings of the New Covenant, or how often the texts of Scripture and Psalms of prayer and thanksgiving, then impressed on the memory, may have guarded against temptation or lightened the burdens and smoothed asperities in the pathway of life, the "Great Day" alone will reveal.*

* Reminiscences of James M'Cachran; of Elder John Ralston; Local Memoranda; Communication from Rev. Mr. McCall; from Samuel Hindman.

THE PARSONAGE.

In Scotland the Manse is considered almost equally essential with the Kirk. As a majority of the ministers of the churches there are not the owners of any means for passing from place to place, it is deemed important that he whose duties require him to be present in the House of God twice or thrice a week should reside near to the scene of his labors.

For many years after the settlement of Presbyterians in America, in consequence of the necessity for every one to be provided with a means of conveyance of his own, parsonages were not considered absolutely essential. The funds of most of the congregations having been exhausted in building a meeting-house and a session-house, no provision was made for a pastor's residence.

This was particularly the case with the churches first established. Hence it often happened that churches whose organization was but yesterday, when compared with those of an early date, were furnished with a dwelling appropriated for the use of the pastor, while the church of which they were in many instances colonies had made no provision of the kind.

Of this the congregation worshipping in this place affords an example. The churches at Coatesville, Waynesburg, and Fairview composed, at first, either wholly or in part of members from this church, had each a parsonage before it was determined to erect one here.

Mr. Black having no family when pastor of the congregation, made his home with some of the members of his charge. The house in which Mr. Dean dwelt in West Nantmeal Township, as stated elsewhere, is no longer in existence, and Mr. Boyd, while supplying the Old Side, continued to reside near his church in Octoraro. Mr. Carmichael, with Scotch thrift and frugality, acquired considerable property, and passed his last years on a farm in West Brandywine Township, which was long the residence of the late Squire M'Clellan. Mr. Nathan Grier, shortly after his marriage, in 1787, bought the farm now belonging to the estate of the late Richard Parke, and resided there until his death. When his son, the Rev. J. N. C. Grier, succeeded him in the pastorate he purchased the homestead, and it continued to be the parsonage until 1841. In that year he erected, on land adjoining the church property, the mansion in which he passed the remainder of his life.

After the resignation of Dr. Grier the necessity of providing a residence for the pastor became so apparent that efforts were made to accomplish it. With the energy and liberality which have always been shown by the members of this Church when they were convinced that any measure was needed for the prosperity of their beloved Zion, funds were collected and a suitable building erected in 1869–'70. The main structure, which is carefully and neatly finished, stands East of the Lower Graveyard, on a part of the land originally owned by the New Side. It is thirty-five feet in front by twenty-six feet deep on the East side; forty-four feet deep on the West side, and two and a half stories in height. The entire cost of the dwelling, out-buildings, and improvement of the ground was about four thousand dollars.

The situation of the parsonage is retired, healthful, and elevated, affording an extensive view in almost every direction, and needs but a tasteful arrangement of the lawn, and the addition of trees and shrubbery, to compare favorably with buildings erected for a similar purpose by rural churches in general.

Like "the ministers' home" in other lands, this parsonage, in the course of years, will become closely connected with the remembrance of the pastors who have occupied it and passed away. Around it associations will gather scarcely less salutary and less solemn than those which pertain to buildings specially dedicated to the service of the Most High.*

* MSS.; Church Records.

SESSION-HOUSES.

As the Presbyterians who first settled in America generally considered the Session-House or Study almost equally important with the Meeting-House, and seldom erected the latter, however rude, without, at the same time, placing the former near by, it is altogether likely that there was a Session-House belonging to the First Meeting-House. But as even tradition is silent respecting such a building, it would be futile to inquire, if it did exist, where it was situated, and whether it served both as a school-house and a place for the meetings of the members of Session.*

The Session-House belonging to the Second Meeting-House stood near the Southeast corner of the ground belonging to Mr. Dean's congregation. It was placed with the front parallel to the Road leading to Downingtown, and was probably furnished with a fireplace. This Session-House having become nearly unfit for use, and being inconveniently situated in respect to the Meeting-House erected in 1761, a log Session-House about sixteen by eighteen feet, with a large fireplace in one end, was built a few rods South of the new church edifice. The entrance was on the side most distant from the church.

This building, like nearly all the Session-Houses of

---

* Some remains of the foundation of what seems to have been a small building, recently noticed near the entrance to the Upper Graveyard, may have been part of a primitive Session-House.

the Presbyterian Church at that day, was used as a school-house. A man by the name of Bowser, who was not remarkable for the purity of his morals or his amiable disposition, taught a school in that Session-House upwards of one hundred years ago. The late John Strong, Major George Dorlan, Nathan Dorlan, Alexander Nesbit, and others whom some now living remember, were among his pupils. Both Bowser and Stephen Wray, who taught towards the close of the last century in the Session-House of the Seceder Meeting-House, were firm believers in the efficacy of the rod. Consequently the frequent applications of it, as an aid to discipline and a spur to mental activity, were a part of their daily programme.

In 1827 the log Session-House was removed, and a stone building about eighteen feet by twenty, with a fireplace in the west end, was erected on the ground occupied by the former Session-House, and stood, like it, with the front to the South. This served for the meetings of the Session until 1875, when it was taken down to afford room for the site of the recently-erected church edifice.

In the construction of the New Meeting-House, a room was set apart in the basement for the transaction of all business belonging to the government of the church. The members of the congregation, therefore, instead of having their Session-House in one place, their Meeting-House in another, and their Sunday-School room at a considerable distance from both, as was formerly the case, have these all conveniently arranged in the same building.*

---

* Local Memoranda; Church Records.

BEQUESTS.

Although there has been a number of wealthy members of the congregation who contributed liberally for benevolent purposes and the keeping of the buildings and enclosures belonging to the church in a proper condition, yet many of them failed to make any provision for assisting to defray the expense of repairs, improvements, and other beneficent objects, after their decease. The bequests, therefore, have been comparatively few and the amount small; the whole sum not exceeding three thousand dollars. This is to be regretted, as not only the cost of preventing the grounds and buildings from becoming impaired, but the purchase of books for the Sunday-Schools, the circulation of tracts and temperance documents, and support of missions require funds which are often difficult to be obtained, and the smallness of which frequently confines these means of doing good within narrow limits.

Those whom the bounty of Providence has blessed with plenty might be the almoners of that bounty when life has ceased by endowments for charitable purposes, the spread of religious intelligence, and the extension of the Redeemer's Kingdom.

BEQUESTS SO FAR AS KNOWN.

Joseph Mackelduff, who died in 1750, left five pounds for the benefit of the Church.

John Beaton, in 1776, bequeathed thirty pounds "for the use of the Meeting-House." This was applied towards defraying the cost of restoring the church edifice after its injury by fire.

Elder William Irwin, whose death occurred in 1794, devised a small sum, six pounds, for the purpose of renewing the fence around the Upper Graveyard.

Hugh Morton, long an active member of the congregation, in 1811 left fifty pounds, which were expended, under the direction of General Stanly, for the iron gate and marble posts at the eastern entrance to the Upper Graveyard.

Isaac Smith directed about one hundred dollars to be placed by his executors in the hands of the trustees of the church to be applied towards keeping the Lower Graveyard and the wall surrounding it in suitable order. A portion of this sum was used to purchase the gate and the pillars that bear the initials of his name which are placed at the entrance, and the balance appropriated towards paying for the repairs and extension of the wall in 1860.

About one hundred and fifty dollars were directed by the will of John Craig, in 1825, to be invested by the trustees of the church, and the interest applied from time to time in keeping the Lower Graveyard in good repair. A part of this was expended for the extension of the enclosure on the South side, and the remainder (two hundred and twelve dollars) in restoring and flagging the wall.

Peter Kurtz, who died March 19, 1880, left five hundred dollars for the benefit of the church, and a like amount was devised for the same purpose by Mrs. Elizabeth Christman, whose death took place in February of the same year.

Mrs. Mary Ann Grier directed in her last Will and Testament that five hundred dollars should be invested by the trustees of the church, and the interest expended in keeping up the graves of herself and her husband, Elder James K. Grier. She also bequeathed five hundred dollars to aid the operations of the church.

A bequest of one hundred dollars was made by Augustus J. Dowlin, who died in April, 1884.

About one hundred and fifty dollars were devised by Thomas Lomas, whose decease occurred in 1883, for keeping the Lower Graveyard in repair.

By the will of William Moore, his executors were directed to place five hundred dollars in the hands of the trustees, a part of it, or the interest accruing, to be expended in keeping his family burial-lots in repair, and the balance to be expended for the benefit of the church.

The sums devised by Mrs. Kurtz, Mrs. Christman, and Mrs. Grier, together amounting to fifteen hundred dollars, less the collateral inheritance tax, were used for the payment of debts arising from the improvement of the enclosures and other necessary expenses connected with the church property.*

* Records of Session; Local Memoranda; Office of Register of Wills.

PEW-HOLDERS IN 1792-96.

In no part of the world are changes of residence more frequent than in the United States. New fields for adventure are continually being laid open. New enterprises which promise much are again and again presented, and real or fancied advantages foster the desire "to better their circumstances," which seems to be the leading idea in the minds of a large portion of our countrymen. As a consequence many abandon the homes of their childhood, and the places where their youthful years were passed, for more inviting and distant localities.

Although this "disposition to wander" is more characteristic of the Scotch-Irish, the Irish, and their posterity, than of any class of our citizens, yet an examination of the following list of pew-holders will show that a considerable number of the supporters of this church at the present time are the descendants of those who sustained a Gospel ministry here fourscore and ten years ago.

All whose names are comprised in this list, and with a few exceptions the generation which immediately succeeded them, are *dead*, but the Church still *lives*.

The influence of their example and of their pious instruction has reached to the third and even to the fourth generation. How much of encouragement does this afford to those who are "never weary in well-doing," and especially to those who have aided in the construction of the building which has recently been dedicated to the service of the Great Head of the church.

They, like their fathers and forefathers, are leaving a memorial of their good works and an influence, which will be seen and felt long after the "places which now know, shall know them no more."

The following is a list of the pew-holders in 1792–96, as near as can be ascertained from imperfect Church Records and other sources:

John Alford.
Ephraim Allen.
James Anderson.
Margaret Anderson.
William Anderson.
Andrew Barr.
Robert Beatty.
William Blair.
William Brown.
Hannah Buchanan.
John Buchanan.
Matthew Buchanan.
Samuel Byers, Sr.
Samuel Byers.
Widow Byers.
Adam Campbell.
David Carson.
Samuel Caruthers.
John Craige.
Samuel Craige.
Parmenas Crowe.
Samuel Cunningham, Esq.
Isaac Davis.
Joshua Davis.
Methusaleh Davis.
David Denny.
James Denny.
Samuel Denny.
William Denny.
William Diven.
George Dorlan.
Nathan Dorlan.
Samuel Dorlan.
John Dunlap.
James Dunwoodie.
John Dunwoodie.
Elizabeth Elliott.
William Elliott.
Theophilus Erwin.
Elizabeth Ferguson.
James Forrest.
Francis Gardner.
Dr. Isaac Gibson.
James Graham.
Michael Graham.
John Gray.

John Grier.
Joseph Grier.
Rev. Nathan Grier.
Adam Guthrie.
James Guthrie.
Agnes Henderson.
William Henderson.
James Hood.
Sarah Hughes.
William Hunter, Esq.
Ezekiel Irwin.
Adam Jack.
John Johnson.
Robert Johnson.
Mary Kennedy.
Samuel Kennedy.
Thomas Kennedy.
William Kennedy.
John Lewis.
William Loag.
Alexander Lockhart, Esq.
James Lockhart, Sr.
James Lockhart.
William Lockhart.
William Long.
Alexander Marshall.
James McCachran.
James McConnel.
Samuel Mackelduff.
James M'Clune.
Benjamin McClure.

James McClure.
Joseph McClure.
Bryan McCune.
Elizabeth McKinly.
Paul McKnight.
James Miller.
David Moore.
James Moore, Esq.
William Moore.
William Moore, Jr.
Hugh Morton.
William Neely.
Robert Nesbit.
David Pittsford.
Charles Reed.
David Robeson.
James Robinson.
John Robison.
Matthias Shoenar.
Col. Robert Smith.
Andrew Stanly.
Matthew Stanly, Esq.
William Sterrett, Sr.
William Sterrett, Jr.
John Todd.
John Strong.
James Tarrance.
Rachel White.
John Winans.
Jonathan Wynn.

TEMPERANCE SOCIETIES.

The Lectures of Dr. Lyman Beecher and others had directed public attention in New England to the increase of intemperance, and measures had been adopted to arrest its progress before any means were devised to stay its ravages in the Middle States. The first Temperance Society was formed in Boston, February 13, 1826, and some years later a few associations having the same object in view, were formed in Pennsylvania.

The first Temperance Society within the bounds of this congregation, and among the earliest organized in Chester County, was formed in 1831. Towards the close of April in that year, a number of residents in the neighborhood assembled for that purpose, in what was long known by the name of Walker's School-House, near the village of Rockville. The meeting was organized by calling the Rev. Dr. J. N. C. Grier to the chair, and the appointment of Master John W. Pinkerton as Secretary. After some remarks by the Chairman, and an interchange of views on the subject, a Temperance Society was formed and a constitution adopted and signed, pledging those whose names were appended* to abstain from making, selling, or using intoxicating liquors.

* See Appendix J.

Of the twenty-eight who then came forward and avowed their determination to aid in lessening or removing the manifold evils of intemperance, twenty-six are dead. Some of them were men whose heads were whitened by the frosts of time, and who had long witnessed and deplored the direful consequences arising from the use of spirituous liquors. Others were men of middle age, around whom families were clustering, and who desired to guard their households against a fruitful source of poverty and disgrace. The majority, however, were young men about to go forth to meet the trials and temptations which beset the pathway of life, and who wisely girded themselves with the armor of total abstinence before they engaged in the conflict.

So far as is known no one violated the obligations entered into on that day, while some of them advocated temperance, both orally and through the medium of the press, with ability and faithfulness.

Meetings were held and addresses on the subject delivered for several years, but although much good was accomplished the enthusiasm subsided, the most active workers became gradually dispersed, and the Society as a distinct organization ceased to exist.

Before closing an account of the first temperance society, it ought to be stated that the use, or more correctly the abuse, of intoxicating liquors was, at that time, far different from what it now is. Then, a laborer would refuse employment unless he received a morning dram, and a building could scarcely be erected or a harvest gathered without the use of ardent spirits. Even aged and otherwise respectable men often found it difficult to preserve a steady gait when returning from vendues, elections, or other public gatherings. The smoke of five distilleries daily rose within the bounds of this congregation, and to get drunk occasionally was scarcely a disgrace.

In 1851 a meeting for the furtherance of temperance was held at Howard Academy, Rockville, and a society formed, of which Elder John Ralston was chosen President. A large number signed the pledge. Public meetings were frequently held, and addresses delivered by the Rev. Dr. J. N. C. Grier, Dr. Lehman, Dr. Hotchkin, Dr. A. K. Gaston, Rev. George Chandler, Rev. William W. Latta, the Principal, and some of the leading students of Howard Academy. Finally, however, this society, like its predecessor of twenty years before, was permitted to languish and die, but not until, through the influence of it and kindred associations, the distillation of ardent spirits in Chester County had ceased, and intoxicating liquors were no longer furnished to those employed in the workshop or the field.*

---

* Local Memoranda; Records of Howard Academy; Personal Reminiscences.

A LIST

OF SUBSCRIBERS TO THE FUND FOR ENCLOSING THE GRAVEYARDS BY A STONE WALL, IN 1794-95.

A.

Ephraim Allen.
Hugh Anderson.
Margaret Anderson.
William Anderson.

B.

Eleanor Barker.
Robert Beatty.
Samuel Beatty.
Sarah Brown.
Thomas Brown.
William Brown.
Samuel Byers.
Samuel Byers, Jr.
Widow Byers.
John Buchanan.
Matthew Buchanan.

C.

Hugh Calhoun.
Adam Campbell.
John Campbell.
David Carson.
Robert Carson.
Mary Carswell.
William Christy.
John Craige.

Robert & Samuel Craige.
William Culberson.
Samuel Cunningham.
William Cunningham.

D.

John Darlington.
Joseph Darlington.
Isaac Davis.
Methusaleh Davis.
David Denny.
William Denny.
George Dorlan.
Nathan Dorlan.
Joseph Dougan.
Daniel Dunlap.
James Dunwoody.
John Dunwoody.

E.

Margaret Elliott.
William Elliott.
Thomas Ewing.

F.

Widow Ferguson.
Andrew Forbis.
John Forbis.

James Forrest.
James Fritz.

G.

Alexander Gillipsie.
Peter Graham.
John Gray.
Dr. Isaac Gibson.
Mrs. Goudey.
Rev. Nathan Grier.
John Grier.
Joseph Grier.
Adam Guthrie.
James Guthrie.
William Guthrie.

H.

Jacob Happersett.
Abram Harler.
Henry Harler.
William Henderson.
James Hood.
Sarah Hughes.
William Hunter, Esq.
James Hutcheson.

I.

John Irwin, Jr.
Mary Irwin.
Theophilus Irwin.
Thomas Irwin.
William Irwin.

J.

Elizabeth Jack.
David Jones.
John Jones.

K.

William Kennedy.
Samuel Kennedy.
George Kennedy.

L.

John Lewis.
Mrs. Lewis.
Joseph Leviston.
William Long.
Alexander Lockhart.
James Lockhart.
William Lockhart.

M.

Richard Mather.
Patrick Maitland.
Samuel Maitland.
William Maitland.
Samuel Mackelduff.
Alexander Marshal.
James McCachran.
Benjamin McClure.
James McClure.
Joseph McClure.
James McConnel.
Alexander M'Conaughy.
Patrick McRahey.
Jane M'Crosky.
David McCrony.
Samuel McCullough
Bryan McCune.
John McFarland.
James McGugan.
Samuel McKinly.
Paul McKnight.
James Miller.
James Moore.

William Moore.
James Morton.

N.

James Neely.
William Neely.
James Nesbit.
Robert Nesbit.

P.

Stephen Pattup.
Joseph Parker.
Mark Peelor.
Isaac Phillips.
Nathaniel Porter.

R.

Charles Reed.
David Robeson.
Hugh Robeson.
James Robeson.
John Robinson.
Nathaniel Robinson.
William Robeson.
John Root.

S.

Andrew Stanly.
Matthew Stanly.
Daniel Shenky.
Widow Sherer.
James Steen.
William Sterrett.
Robert Sterrett.
John Smith.
John Smith, Jr.
Colonel Robert Smith.
William Story.

T.

Widow Thompson.

W.

Robert Wallace.
Jacob Waters.
John Walker.
Aaron White.
Widow White.
Nancy Wilson.
William Wilson.
Alexander Wilson.
John Winance.
Jonathan Wynn.

LEGISLATORS.

Legislators who resided within the bounds of the congregation.*

MEMBERS OF CONGRESS.

Robert Jenkins was a Member from 1807 to 1811. Two terms.
David Potts   "   "   " 1831 to 1839. Four terms.
Abraham McIllvaine   "   " 1843 to 1849. Three terms.

MEMBERS OF STATE LEGISLATURE.

Col. Robert Smith was a Member in 1785.
James Moore, Esq.,   "   " 1788.
Col. Thomas Bull   " from 1793 to 1802.
Methusaleh Davis   " in 1802, 1803, 1804, 1805, and 1806.
Gen. Matthew Stanly   " " 1829.
Jesse James, Esq.,   " " 1829, 1851, and 1852.
Dr. Benjamin Griffith   " " 1830, 1831, and 1832.
Bernard Way, Esq.,   " " 1835.
Abraham McIlvane   " " 1836 and 1837.
Col. Thomas K. Bull   " " 1846, 1847, and 1848.
James M. Dorlan   " " 1850.
Andrew Buchanan   " " 1855.
Morton Garrett   " " 1857.
Capt. Levi Fetters   " " 1883 and 1885.

---

* State and Congressional Records.

PHYSICIANS.

It is a matter of surprise and regret to every one, when examining the annals of the past, to find that so little has been placed on record of physicians, and especially of those who practised in rural districts. While much that is noteworthy in the lives of clergymen, members of the bar, legislators, and military men has been preserved, materials for biographical notices of physicians, for the most part, must be sought by the dim light of tradition or gathered from the fading recollection of friends who have survived them. This is particularly the case with those who have practised medicine within the bounds of this congregation.

The earliest whose name has reached the present time is Dr. Thomas Rheese, who appears to have been engaged as a physician previous to the middle of the last century and some years afterwards.

Dr. Rheese was succeeded by Dr. John Flavel Carmichael, a son of the Rev. John Carmichael, and Dr. Joseph Gardner, a son of Elder Francis Gardner. Dr. Carmichael followed his profession in the bounds of his father's congregation until 1788, when he entered the Army of the United States as a surgeon. Dr. Gardner was engaged principally in the southern and western portions of Mr. Carmichael's charge. In 1790, he removed to Maryland. He acquired a high reputation as a physician, and his professional engagements extended over a large area.

About 1780, Dr. Thomas Harris, who was much esteemed for his medical skill, commenced the practice of his profession at Indian-town, in Wallace Township. He seems, after the removal of Dr. Carmichael and Dr. Gardner, to have had no competitor nearer than Dr. Sturgis, of Downingtown.

Dr. Thomas Kennedy, the friend and pupil of Dr. Harris, succeeded to his practice in 1796 or '97. Dr. Kennedy soon became noted for his skill and attention to his patients. His practice consequently embraced a large extent of country. Several years before his death, in April, 1814, he was the only resident physician within the bounds of the Rev. Nathan Grier's charge.*

Dr. John E. Grier, a graduate of Dickinson College and of the University of Pennsylvania, began the practice of medicine in 1813. Being well educated and having a good reputation as a surgeon, he was largely patronized. Dr. Grier remained until about 1825, when he removed to the State of Ohio. He took up his residence in the Miami Valley, where and in other parts of that State, he remained until his death, in 1844.

In 1814, Dr. Benjamin Griffith began the practice of medicine near Glen Moore, and continued in the active discharge of his professional duties upwards of forty-four years. He died May 12, 1858. Unas-

---

* Dr. Todd was practising in West Brandywine Township in 1800, but in what part or how long, the writer has been unable to learn.

suming and attentive to those who needed medical aid, Dr. Griffith was much esteemed as a physician and respected as a friend and a neighbor.

Dr. John M'Calmont, who, in 1810, settled near Waynesburg, in the Western part of the congregation, practised with much ability and success until a few years before his death, in 1870. Like his contemporary, Dr. Griffith, he enjoyed the entire confidence of the community.

In 1818, Dr. Isaac Pennington, a well-read physician, who had been a surgeon in the Army of the United States during the last War with England, located a little below Waynesburg. He soon obtained a lucrative practice, which he retained until his removal, in 1832, to one of the Southern States. After an absence of several years he returned, and remained in the practice of his profession until his death, near Compassville, May 6, 1849.

Dr. Joseph F. Grier, a younger brother of Elder James K. Grier, finished his medical studies in 1828. Dr. Grier erected the building lately owned by Mrs. Agnes Happersett, in which he resided and gave the community the benefit of his medical skill, until the Fall of 1837. He then removed to Lewisburg, Union County, where he continued in the discharge of his professional duties until a short time before his death, in February, 1858.

About three years after the withdrawal of Dr. Grier, Dr. A. K. Gaston removed from Easton, Pa., to where he lately resided, and engaged in the practice of medicine. Being not only an able physician, but also a gentleman of general culture, he was soon in the enjoyment of an extensive practice, which he retained until his death, December 22, 1882.

Dr. Nathan G. Thompson, eldest son of the late Dr. Thompson, a prominent physician of Fagg's Manor, commenced the study of medicine with Dr. A. K. Gaston, and after his graduation, February 28, 1852, engaged in the practice of his profession, in which he has been eminently successful. He is now the principal physician actively engaged within the bounds of the congregation.

Dr. Isaac Gibson, about 1786, and Dr. Effinger Happersett, about 1816, commenced the practice of medicine; but as neither of them had received a medical education they were not largely patronized.

Such is a brief record of the laborious, self-denying, and, in many instances, gifted men, who have practised the healing art within the varying bounds of this congregation, during the last hundred and twenty-five years.

It is a meagre and imperfect sketch, but should it be considered strange that it is so, when even the Medical Department of the University of Pennsylvania cannot furnish a complete list of its graduates prior to the beginning of the present century, when degrees began to be annually conferred?*

---

* MS. Collections.

GRAVEYARDS.

Owing to their situation at a different level along the Turnpike Road, the graveyards belonging to this church were named accordingly; the one South of that Road being generally known by the name of the Upper Graveyard, while the one North of the same highway is usually called the Lower Graveyard.

UPPER GRAVEYARD.

Shortly after the erection of the first Meeting-House, a piece of land immediately to the East of that building was appropriated for a burial-place. This continued to be used as THE graveyard until that Meeting-House was abandoned. The burial-ground was then enlarged, chiefly by extending it towards the South and East, and enclosed by a board fence. In 1794 or 1795 it was again enlarged, and the board fence replaced by a stone wall.

The entrance, which was on the North side, next to the public Road, remained there until 1822, when the marble posts and iron gate, still in use, were procured by the late General Matthew Stanly. The entrance was then placed where it now is, on the Eastern side of the burial-ground, and near to the church building.

In 1853, mainly through the exertions of Elder James K. Grier, another addition was made to this graveyard. The wall was also repaired, and a gateway placed on the Southwestern side.

At present this burial-place is an irregular six-sided plot of ground, containing about two acres, and from the dryness of the soil and the absence of substances which render excavation difficult, is admirably adapted to the purpose.

For upwards of three-quarters of a century after it had been set apart as a burial-ground, the remains of a suicide were not permitted to be interred within its limits. But the custom, derived from a barbarous age, of denying the usual rites of burial to those who had died by their own hand, gave place to more enlightened and Christian sentiments.

The first lettered headstones placed in this yard are those at the graves of Mrs. Jane Sterling and the infant children of Mr. Carmichael, although they were not the first persons buried within this enclosure. These stones were prepared at Burlington, N. J., then the rival of Philadelphia.*

Until a recent period no record of the interments was kept, and many of those buried there sleep without even an unlettered stone to mark their last resting-place.† It is, therefore, impossible to ascertain how many have been buried in this graveyard. Taking the average at twenty-five annually,—and some years it was much greater,—the whole number cannot be less

---

* The oldest tombstones are those which cover the remains of the first proprietor of Springton Forge, Robert M'Conaughy, and of his wife and son. The first monument, except a very small one, was erected about 1840, by General Stanly, in memory of his wife.

† See Appendix R.

than three thousand five hundred. Among them are the remains of the Rev. John Carmichael, the Rev. Nathan Grier, the Rev. John W. Grier, the Rev. J. N. C. Grier, D.D., of more than twenty who were Ruling Elders in this church, and of several who fought, and some who fell in the Revolutionary and other national conflicts.

Unfortunately, no plan has been followed in the interments, each member of the congregation having, in most instances, selected his family burial-place as he thought proper, and therefore the attraction which regularity would have added to the naturally beautiful site cannot be obtained.

This burial-ground is now furrowed with graves and white with the memorials which affection has placed to perpetuate the names and the virtues of the departed, and only a few years can pass before another addition to it will be required.[*] But whatever the extension may be, or however great the number which will be laid there to await the Second Coming of the Son of Man, we have 'the pleasing assurance that it will never be desecrated. The recent erection of a large and costly Meeting-House adjoining it, and the determination which has been shown by the present members of the congregation to keep the fire continually burning which was kindled on the altar in the wilderness by their forefathers, are guarantees for its preservation. No greedy owner of ad-

---

[*] It has recently been enlarged by an extension south. The new enclosure has been laid out in lots and arranged in accordance with the plan of modern cemeteries.

jacent land will be permitted to call it his own, nor the hand of an unfeeling husbandman be allowed to remove the memorials of the departed, and change places, often wet by the tears of sorrow and affection, into cultivated fields. That such an event might occur may seem to many the offspring of a highly-wrought imagination. An examination, however, would show them that covetousness and vandalism have removed every trace of several graveyards which belonged to Presbyterian Churches established at an early period in Lancaster, Berks, Dauphin, and other counties.

LOWER GRAVEYARD.

When those who withdrew from Mr. Black's congregation and placed themselves under the direction of the Synod of New Brunswick built their Meeting-House, they set apart a portion of the land which they had obtained for a burial-ground, and it is still used for that purpose. Among the first interred in this graveyard was their lamented pastor, the Rev. William Dean. The tombstone which covers his remains was probably placed there several years after his death. There are circumstances which lead to the conclusion that his age is incorrectly stated. It bears an earlier date than any memorial stone in either graveyard.

This graveyard, which occupies a rectangular space of about half an acre, was enclosed by a stone wall in 1796. It has remained without any enlargement, except a small extension on the Southern side in 1860, when the wall was also repaired and capped with flag-stones.

In 1821 the iron gate and marble posts at the entrance were placed there, in accordance with the will of Isaac Smith, who also left a small sum for the purpose of keeping the yard and its surroundings in a proper condition.

Like the Upper Graveyard, this burial-ground possesses the advantages of dryness of soil and of freedom from obstructions beneath the surface; but owing, probably, to its greater distance from the Church building, the interments in it have been much fewer than in the other burial-place.

The Lower Graveyard, the Meeting-House which then stood near it, and the whole of the ground, for which payment was made by Mr. Dean only the May before his death, became after the Union the property of the United Congregation. It, together with the land previously obtained, still remains in the possession of the Church.*

* Local Memoranda; Reminiscences of aged Residents.

MISCELLANEOUS ITEMS.

Sixty years ago but four vehicles could be seen at the Manor Meeting-House on the Sabbath, and these were the old-fashioned two-wheeled gig, with leather springs. A majority of the congregation came afoot, the rest on horseback. For convenience in mounting and alighting, "upping blocks" were placed under almost every shade-tree or place suitable for the standing of horses. Fans were commonly used, umbrellas were few, and parasols almost unknown.

The pews until quite a recent period were personal property, and generally owned by those who occupied them on the Sabbath. Sometimes when the owner did not need the whole of his pew, he either sold a part or rented it to those who were unable to obtain sitting, as it was called, elsewhere. On one occasion, the creditors of a man, who had become bankrupt, seized and sold his pew, but instances of such rapacity were rare.

Owing to the nearness of the turnpike road to the meeting-house, the noise occasioned by heavy vehicles passing along the rough highway on the Sabbath was frequently a source of great annoyance. During the period that the turnpike road was the principal route for the transportation of merchandise to Pittsburg and other Western cities, the disturbance caused by the heavily-loaded wagons, often closely following one another, was so great as sometimes to interrupt public worship. A number of the teamsters were arrested and fined for pursuing their occupation on the Lord's Day, but this proceeding rather increased than diminished the evil, as after that many of them made it an object to pass along the road during divine service.

In 1798 the school-house on the church property, on account of its size, and being near to the point where the three townships of West Nantmeal, Honeybrook, and West Brandywine joined, was selected for holding the annual election. As political contests were then conducted with a bitterness and a resort to personal violence now comparatively rare, much occurred on "election day" which ill comported with the sacredness of the place. Fighting was not uncommon. Ardent Democrats and Federalists did not hesitate to use staffs and clubs as "knock-down arguments." The liquor-stands caused the steps of many to become unsteady. Boisterous and profane language was freely used, and altogether a scene was presented in sickening contrast with the precepts of that Gospel at whose advent was proclaimed, Peace on earth and good-will to man. Finally the impropriety of using any of the property belonging to the congregation for a secular purpose which was attended with disorder and contention, became so manifest that another place was selected where the citizens of the three townships could meet, wrangle, and cast their votes.

The salaries of clergymen during many years were low, and after making allowance for the difference in the price of the necessaries of life, when compared with the cost of like articles at the present time, it is often difficult at first sight to understand how they acquired property as many of them did. This difficulty is due to overlooking the fact that the amount promised as salary was but a part, and frequently the smallest part, of what was received. The farmers in the Fall, especially, did not forget to furnish the minister with flour, potatoes, wood, meat, and in some instances material for clothing, sufficient for the greater part of the year; those, too, who expected to call occasionally at the manse, generally included among their gifts a keg of peach-brandy, then a much-esteemed beverage.

Another source of income was marriages. As a marriage performed by a magistrate was generally considered less respectable, and by some less binding than when it was solemnized by a minister, well-known clergymen were called upon to perform the interesting ceremony not only by members of their own congregation, but by many others. On these occasions, although the bride frequently adjusted her attire by the aid of a pail of water as a looking-glass, and the thoughtful bridegroom carried in rude saddle-bags "a bite for the horses" during the delay at the parson's, yet those who rewarded the pastor with less than a one-pound note were commonly regarded as having made a bad start on the road to connubial happiness.

Psalm-books being scarce and some of the congregation being unable to read, the precentor or clerk usually lined the psalm; that is, he read two lines aloud, and when these had been sung, the next two, until the conclusion of the exercise. This manner of conducting the singing was continued long after the necessity for it had ceased. During the pastorate of the Rev. Nathan Grier, Watts's Psalms and Hymns became the text-book, much to the dissatisfaction of the older members of the congregation. This, as is well known, has been forced to give place in many churches to the Hymnal, for what reason is difficult to discover. If the sturdy founders of Presbyterianism and their immediate descendants adhered somewhat tenaciously to an almost literal translation of the inspired anthems of the "man after God's own heart," the Presbyterians of the present day have gone to the opposite extreme in discarding even the title, and to a great extent the songs, of "the sweet singer of Israel."

The names of but a few of those who "led the singing" have been preserved. Mr. Benjamin McClure was precentor during a considerable part of the Rev. Nathan Grier's pastorate. Major George Dorlan also officiated until near his decease, in 1829. He was succeeded by Mr. William Forrest. For more than thirty years the singing was conducted by Elder John Ralston. After the remodelling of the Meeting-House in 1839, the choir was seated in the front of the gallery, instead of at the base of the pulpit The introduction of the choir was considered quite an innovation on time-honored custom, but within the last few years the departure from Puritan simplicity has been further increased by invoking the aid of instrumental music.

It has been said that a Presbyterian Church never dies. While this is true in the main, and especially in Chester County, where the number of Presbyterian

Churches has been nearly doubled during the present century, yet a change in the location of meeting-houses has become manifest. This is seen not only in the erection of buildings for public worship where none previously existed, but also in the replacing of old meeting-houses by new. There being no villages, the first settlers generally erected their church edifices on high ground, and

"The decent church that topped the neighboring hill"

could be seen here as well as in the fatherland. But the march of improvement has caused the new meeting-house in many instances to be placed at a distance from the site occupied by the one first erected. The employment of water-power, the advantage of streams for navigation, and of railways which necessarily pass where the least grade must be overcome, have caused cities and villages to spring up in valleys and low grounds. Hence new meeting-houses, whenever it can be done, are placed where easiness of access by the present means of travel is most readily obtained. This change of site, while it has often been a means of increasing the number in attendance, and in some instances has saved weak churches from being disbanded, has also caused a neglect of the graveyard connected with the first meeting-house. New burial-places are sought, and the enclosure where the remains of the founders of the church were laid is too frequently left with no Old Mortality to restore the time-worn epitaphs on its tombstones, or Nehemiah to rebuild the broken-down walls of the "city of the dead."

Before the Revolution, and years afterward, the cocked hat, knee-breeches, and silver shoe-buckles extending across the foot were the favorite costume of the elderly and middle-aged gentlemen of the congregation. The hat was three-cornered, one corner being on each side in front, and another usually adorned with a tassel behind. As breeches left the part extending from the knee to the ankle exposed, those who were not furnished with well-proportioned limbs frequently attempted to remedy the defect by placing a pad or bandage on the back part of the exposed member. But this, like many attempts at improvement, sometimes failed. The pad would become displaced and mar the appearance, instead of adding to the proportions of the part which it was intended to aid. The face was close shaven, but a part of the hair of the head was allowed to acquire its full length. This was plaited or surrounded by a ribbon and permitted to hang down the back. It was not unlike the Chinese appendage euphoniously styled a pig-tail, except that it depended from the back of the head instead of from the top. As the hair in the queue, as it was called, required oiling occasionally, in the course of time it imparted a shining appearance to the upper part of the well-worn coat.

The ladies generally attended meeting dressed in a short gown not unlike the modern sacque, and another article of dress which has given the prefix to the government of those ladies who usurp the control of the household. On this part of the attire the most care was bestowed, and the variety and brilliancy of its colors was often the pride of the wearer. The hair which was not permitted to fall over the back, was covered by a sufficiently capacious, plain bonnet, which added to instead of detracting from the modesty of the wearer. Rings on the fingers were not common, and appendages from the ears were rarely seen. Even after these fashions, derived from the fatherland, had passed away, almost every one was attired in clothing of domestic manufacture. The "Sunday suit" was made to last as long as possible, and when it had been obtained by those who had not reached their full growth, the care with which it had been preserved was shown by its failure to cover a portion of the arms and lower extremities of the wearer.

From the organization of the Church until the establishment of Sunday-Schools rendered them, in a measure, unnecessary, public examinations of the children whose parents belonged to the congregation were annually made by the pastor. These examinations, directed mainly to ascertaining the familiarity of the young with the Shorter Catechism, and their knowledge of religious truth, were occasions of interest and benefit to both the children and their parents. The latter being forcibly reminded of the duties devolving upon them, and the former aided in becoming acquainted with the Scriptures and the doctrines taught and maintained by the Presbyterian Church.

After the ingathering of the Summer crops, a day was appointed to return thanks for the blessings of plenty and the fulfilment of the promise that seed-time and harvest should never fail. The day of the month was not always the same, but the day of the week was invariably Thursday. Why Thursday and no other day was selected is difficult to ascertain. It is most likely connected with some of those lingering superstitions respecting lucky and unlucky days which held such a conspicuous place in heathen mythology, and which have not been entirely banished from Christian communities. The number is not so small as many suppose who still regard Friday as an unlucky day, and it is but recently that the execution of criminals ceased to be ordered on that day of the week exclusively. It was probably owing to the custom of the Puritans and Presbyterians that Governors of States and the Chief Magistrate of the Union* have always selected Thursday for the day of State and National thanksgiving. The custom so becoming an agricultural community of appointing a thanksgiving after the harvest has been gathered is still observed by the congregation.

The Communion was held twice a year, in May and in October. The Sabbath immediately preceding the administration of the ordinances was called the preparation Sabbath. On Friday of the same week, which was commonly observed as a Fast Day, there were religious exercises, and also on Saturday and Monday. On the Sacrament Sabbath some pastor of a neighboring congregation usually assisted, and after a sermon by the minister in charge the sacrament was administered. The communicants seated themselves at tables placed in the aisles, and, as the number was generally

---

* A national thanksgiving was appointed by President Lincoln in 1863, and his example has been followed by each of his successors. A thanksgiving was first appointed by the Governor of Pennsylvania in 1843.

too large to be seated at one table, those first seated, after the elements had been served, retired, and others took their places, so that there were frequently three or four tables. Every one entitled to participate was furnished with a token, as it was called. This was a small square piece of lead with the letter C (Communicant) stamped upon it. These were taken up by the members of the Session after those desiring to commune had seated themselves in the aisle. Before commencing to serve the tables, an invitation was always given by the pastor to those who were in good standing in other orthodox denominations to unite with the members of his charge in commemorating the suffering and death of their common Saviour.

During the division of the Presbyterian Church into Old and New School, Dr. Grier and his congregation remained with the Old Side. Unlike the schism of 1741, the division of 1837 was a division of churches, but rarely of congregations.

In 1838 the Meeting-House was broken into, and the Communion Service, hymn-books, and whatever could be conveniently carried were taken, and the furniture damaged. The perpetrators of the sacrilege were never detected.

For sixty years after the erection of the Meeting-House the congregation was dependent for water on a spring several hundred yards distant. In 1794, chiefly through the exertions of the Rev. Nathan Grier, a well was sunk near the church building. As the situation is elevated and the well consequently deep, it was used for upwards of a quarter of a century as a draw-well.

It is worthy of notice that last year a long-needed improvement was made by the erection, at a cost of but little exceeding one thousand dollars, of thirty-five sheds, each nine feet by twenty, for the sheltering of horses and vehicles.

That the first settlers were consistent members of the church, and esteemed by their neighbors and acquaintances in their native land, is shown by the following certificate, which is a specimen of many that were brought by those who came to America to better their circumstances and enjoy the liberty to worship God without "let or hindrance":

> Whereas the bearers here of John long & his wife design for America, these are to Certifie that they have lived in this Congregation the most part of their time and still behaved themselves Soberly, and now at their departure from hence are free of all publick Scandall known to us. as wittness my hand this 8th of July 1736.
>
> SAM^L DUNLAP.
>
> LETTERKENNY, IRELAND.

This closes an imperfect history of a church which during one hundred and fifty years has been a beacon-light guiding to the haven of eternal safety. When those who attend the weekly services of its sanctuary shall meet to celebrate the three hundreth anniversary of the organization of a church in this portion of Zion, one hundred and fifty years will have been added to the list of centuries, and all now living, their children, and their children's children will have made the pilgrimage journey from the cradle to the grave.

That long interval now the unwritten future will then be the recorded past. A past in which they will devoutly recognize, as we do, the guiding hand of the God of their fathers. A past which will contain many memorials of faithful pastors, of sincere worshippers, and of sons and daughters of the church who aided in diffusing the cheering light of the Gospel in the now benighted regions of Asia, Africa, and the Islands of the Ocean.

APPENDIX.

A.

To all Charitable and well Disposed Persons to whom thes presents may Come:

THE PETITION OF THE PRESBYTERIAN CONGREGATION IN THE FORKS OF BRANDYWINE

Humbly showeth: That your petitioners have lately ben brought as a Society, into afflictive and Trying Circumstances, By our Meeting house, an excellent and Commodious billding Beeing Reduced to ashes, Shortly after the Death of our Revd Pastor—We wish to have the public worship of God, Decently and Profitable Conducted amonghst us, in order to which the Erection of a house of Worship is Necessary. But by reason of the Scarcity of Cash; and the Several heave taxes we have paid and have To pay we ar Rendered unable to attain that valuable object without the assistance of our Christian Brethren in other places. We must hope for Success in our address to the Inhabitants of a Christian Country who know that Charity and compassion to the afflicted is the very Image of the Saviour, that God loveth a cheerful Giver and promiseth that those who Caste their Bread on the waters, shall find it after many Days: We therefore Relying on your Goodness and Generosity most Respectfully and Humbly request your kind assistance.

Signed in the Name of the Society By us the Trustees of the Congregation.

SAMUEL CUNNINGHAM,	DAVID DENNY,
JNO. CULBERTSON,	JAS. DUNWODIES,
JAS. MCCLURE,	WILLIAM ANDERSON,
ROBT. LOCKHART.	

FORKS OF BRANDYWINE, March 7, 1786.

B.

CEREMONIES AT THE LAYING OF THE CORNER-STONE OF THE NEW CHURCH EDIFICE, AUGUST 7, 1875.

The exercises were opened with an impressive prayer by the Rev. J. N. C. Grier, D.D.; a Historical Sketch of the Church, prepared by a former member, was then read by the pastor, Mr. McColl, and short addresses delivered by the Rev. Messrs. Roberts, Tothcroth, Hollifield, and Collier, pastors of the Churches organized originally either wholly or in part by members of the Manor Church.

The Box deposited in the Corner-Stone contained a copy of the New Testament, a Hymn-Book, Historical Sketch above mentioned, Historical Discourse, and Semi-Century Sermon of Dr. Grier, a list of the Church Officers, the Act of Incorporation, and specimens of the Silver Coins struck in 1875, presented by ex-Governor Pollock, Director of the United States Mint, the different Postage-Stamps, a Letter and Postal Card to our Children's Children, and a copy of each of the following periodicals: *The Presbyterian Weekly, Presbyterian Banner, Woman's Work for Woman, The Village Record, Jeffersonian, Daily Local,* and *North American Gazette.**

C.

PLAN OF SCHOOL AT NEW LONDON.

ESTABLISHED IN 1744 BY THE SYNOD OF PHILADELPHIA.

1. That all persons who please may send their children and have them instructed gratis in the languages, philosophy, and divinity.

2. That the school be supported by yearly contributions from the congregations under their care.

3. That if any funds remain after paying the salaries of the Master and Tutor, they shall be expended in the purchase of books and other necessaries for the school.

---

* Church Records; Local Memoranda.

APPENDIX.

The Rev. Francis Allison, D.D.,* subsequently Vice-Provost of the University of Pennsylvania, and the successor of Andrews as pastor of the First Presbyterian Church, who had opened an Academy near the village three years before, was appointed Master at a yearly salary of 20£ ($53.33⅓) Pennsylvania Currency.

This school became justly celebrated. Besides furnishing the church with well-educated ministers, it afforded instruction to many who became eminent as statesmen and scholars. Among its pupils were Charles Thomson, Secretary of the Continental Congress, and author of a translation of the New Testament remarkable for its fidelity; Rev. John Ewing, D.D., Provost of the University of Pennsylvania; David Ramsay, the Historian; Hugh Williamson, M.D., LL.D., a distinguished patriot and miscellaneous writer; Rev. James Latta, D.D., an eminent divine and teacher; George Reed and James Smith, signers of the Declaration of Independence; Thomas McKean, nine years Governor of Pennsylvania, and one of the seven natives of Chester County on whom the honorary degree of LL.D. has been conferred.

Although the school was under Presbyterian control, it afforded *gratuitous* instruction of a high order to all denominations alike.†

---

* Dr. Allison died November 28, 1779, and his remains were interred in the burial-ground adjoining the First Presbyterian Meeting-House erected in Pennsylvania. That Meeting-House, commonly known by the name of Old Buttonwood, stood at the Southeast corner of Bank and Market Streets, Philadelphia. It was built in 1704, rebuilt in 1794, abandoned and sold in 1821-22. The burial-ground remained until about 1840, when the dead of a hundred years were removed and its site occupied by warehouses. The first Presbyterian Church in America was built at Snowhill, Md., in 1685.

† Minutes of Synod of Philadelphia; Rev. R. Dubois, "Hist. New London Pres. Church;" "Biography of Eminent Pennsylvanians."

D.

COMMENDATORY LETTER GIVEN ADAM BOYD BY COTTON MATHER.

Boston, N. E., June 10, 1724.

Our worthy friend, Mr. Adam Boyd, being on a return to Europe, it is hereby certified on his behalf, that for the years of his late sojourning in these parts of the world, his behavior, so far as we understand, has been inoffensive and commendable, and such as hath justified the testimonials with which he arrived hither. And we make no doubt that he will make a report of the kind reception which he and others of his and our brethren coming from Scotland and Ireland hither (whereof more than two or three are at this time acceptably exercising their ministry in our churches), have found in this country, that will be very contrary to the misrepresentations which some disturbers of the peace have given of it.

We implore the blessing of our gracious Lord upon his person and his voyage and hope that wherever he may be disposed of, he may have the rewards and comforts of a patient continuance in well doing to attend him.

E.

NAMES OF THOSE WHO SUBSCRIBED FOR THE SUPPORT OF MR. BOYD WHILE HE WAS PASTOR OF THE CHURCH IN THE FORKS OF BRANDYWINE.

COPIED FROM HIS MEMORANDUM BOOK BY REV. A. B. CROSS.

Name.	When Subscription was made.	When it ceased.
John Henderson	Aug. 11, 1741	1757
James Wilson	" "	1758
Joseph Mackelduff	" "	1750

"Paid to his death," in September, 1750. "His brother, Samuel, paid up until 1757."

APPENDIX.

Name.	When Subscription was made.	When it ceased.
Francis Long	Aug. 11, 1741	1752
Paid until 1752. The last two or three years by his brother Joseph, he being dead.		
William Dunbar	" "	1746
"When he moved over the river" (the Susquehannah).		
Samuel McKinly	" "	1758
Edward Irwin	" "	1756
"Paid by his widow to 1756."		
Robert Irwin	" "	1758
"Paid by his widow to 1758."		
Patrick Lockhart	" "	1758
"Paid by his widow to 1758."		
John Bryan	" "	1758
"Paid by his widow to 1758."		
John McDermid	" "	1758
"Paid by his widow to 1758."		
Francis Alexander	" "	1758
David Denny	" "	1758
"Subscription doubled last five years."		
Abraham M'Connell	" "	1751
"Moved over the Susquehanna."		
William Erwin	" "	
"Increased his subscription in 1749 and '50. Moved over the River."		
James Stewart	" "	1758
John Dunwoody	" "	1758
William Wilson	" "	
"October, 1747, moved with his friends to Virginia."		
Robert Steel	" "	
"Moved out of place."		
James Porter	" "	1757
Samuel Carroll	" "	1750
"Moved to Virginia."		
Andrew Donaldson	" "	1758

Name.	When Subscription was made.	When it ceased.
James Mitchell	Aug. 11, 1741	1749
"Moved to Virginia."		
Joseph Carroll	" "	1755
"Moved to Carolina."		
George Irwin	" "	1757
George Gordon	" "	1747
"Moved October, 1748."		
Andrew Wilson	" "	1758
John White	" "	1758
James Love	" "	1746
"Moved."		
John Long	" "	1757
Paid by publications and riddles,* except one year, until 1757.		
John Little	" "	1753
Matthew McKorkell	" "	1746
Removed to Leacock.		

The above Thirty-one subscribers appear to have been those who guaranteed to Mr. Boyd the Salary of Twenty Pounds, when he took charge of the congregation in August, 1741.

SUBSEQUENT SUBSCRIPTIONS.

Name.	Commenced.	Ceased.
John Lewis	1742	1758
William Ferguson	1742	1758
George Ahill	Aug. 11, 1744	
"Died." Probably that year.		
John Elliott	Feb. 3, 1745	1757
Joseph Poag	Sept. 1, 1745	1758
Alexander Laverty	Nov. 4, 1745	1746
"Moved."		
George Little	1745	
"Removed."		

---

* The "publications" were notices of marriages, which the law required to be publicly announced when performed by a clergyman. The "riddles" were sieves for winnowing mills.

APPENDIX.

Name.	Commenced.	Ceased.
Francis Gardiner	1745	1757
David Watson	April, 1746	
David Henderson	April 14, 1746	
"In October, 1747, he moved to Virginia."		
Alexander Maclean	April 27, 1746	1757
"Moved to Carolina."		
Mary Darlington	Oct. 1746	1758
William Mains	1746	1750
"Moved to Carolina."		
James Jack	1746	1758
William Irwin	1746	1758
Andrew Wilson, Sen.	1746	1756
"Dead. Family Extinct."		
Dougal McIntire	1746	1752
Thomas Wilson	1746	1757
John Wilson	1746	
"Moved."		
John M'Clure	1746	1753
William Norris	1746	
"Moved."		
Isaac McKinly	1746	1752
"Moved over river."		
John McCorkle	1746	1748
"Moved."		
Hugh McCrary	1746	
"Moved to Virginia."		
Thomas Karson	1746	1751
Elizabeth Graham (widow)	1746	1752
James Scott	1746	1757
Hugh Morrison	1746	1758
James Watson	1746	1748
"Gone to Virginia."		
Robert Woodrow	1746	
"Moved out of Congregation."		
Robert Smith	1747	1758
John McHenry	March, 1747	1757

APPENDIX.

Name.	Commenced.	Ceased.
David Shearer	1747	
"Moved to Middle Octoraro."		
Thomas McNeal	1747	1751
"Moved over the river."		
James Laird	1747	
"Removed."		
James Gibson	1747	1751
"Moved out of Congregation."		
John Gibson	1747	1755
Frederick McCaskie	1747	
Alexander Maxwell	1747	
"Absconded."		

1749.

Name.	Commenced.	Ceased.
William Dunwoody	Sept. 1749	1758
Fraley McKewan	1749	1752
"Moved."		
John Gardiner	1749	1758
James Ross	1749	1758
John Harper	1749	
"Moved to Octoraro."		
Samuel Byers	1749	1757
William Little	1749	1758
James Ross	1750	Nov. 1751
George Ligate	1750	Nov. 1757
Thomas Scott	1750	1756
John Bell	1750	1754
Hugh Shearer	1750	1752
Jane Jennings	May, 1750	1751
William Ratchford	Nov. 1750	1751
"Moved to Carolina."		
John McFarlane	1750	1752
George Robison	Oct. 1750	June, 1753

1751.

Name.	Commenced.	Ceased.
Ludwick Ligate	April 26, 1751	1758
Cormick McDermond	" "	
"Removed."		

APPENDIX. 239

Name.	Commenced.	Ceased.
Patrick Mairork	April 26, 1751	1755
"He is an apostate."		

1752.

Robert Wilson	1752	1756
Robert Futhey	1752	1758
James Moore	May 24, 1752	
No date given, probably paid until 1758.		
Theophilus Irwin	" " 1752	
No date given, probably paid until 1758.		
Matthew Harbison	1752	
No date given, probably paid until 1758.		
Francis Gardiner, Jr.	1752	
No date given, probably paid until 1758.		
James and Robert McClure	1752	
No date given, probably paid until 1758.		
Joseph Long	1752	1757
James Beatty	1752	
No date given, probably paid until 1758.		

1753.

Thomas Hope	May, 1753	
"Moved over the river."		
Robert Robinson	June 27, 1753	1756
William Ross and Alexander Nesbit	1753	1757
Andrew Spence	1753	1757
"By work, etc., to 1757."		
Thomas Byle	1753	1758
George Campbell	May, 1753	1754
"Moved."		

1754.

William Allan	1754	

1755.

Alexander Gorden	1755	1758
"Part in work."		
James Spence	1755	1757
Robert Robison	Sept. 15, 1755	1757
Alexander Donaldson	May 26, 1755	1758
Probably 1758.		

Name.	Commenced.	Ceased.
Patrick Stewart	May 26, 1755	1756
William Wallace	1755	1758
Probably 1758.		
John Withrow	1755	1758
Probably 1758.		
John Craige	1755	
"One and a half years."		
John Patterson	1755	1758
1756.		
John Smith	May, 1756	1757
Samuel Byers	May 26, 1756	1758

"Robert Piersol paid one year."

"John Young and his brother, Archibald, generally pay me without subscribing." Also Samuel Ross, Samuel Long, "and Thomas Reah."

"Received from the congregation in the Forks of Brandywine all I expected from them."

"My relation to Forks of Brandywine dissolved in a most irregular manner, October, 1758."

It will be observed by the above list that during the last two or three years of Mr. Boyd's pastorate the names added to the list of subscribers for the payment of his salary were few. This was probably owing to the fact that from 1756 or '57, when the "Seceder Meeting-House" was built, three churches,—Mr. Boyd's, the New Side, and the Seceder,—were attempted to be sustained within a short distance of one another.

LIST OF SUBSCRIBERS FOR MR. BOYD'S SALARY AT OCTORARO, SEPTEMBER 1, 1758.

Daniel Henderson.
William Henderson.
Thomas Hope.
John Brewster.
Charles Gilkie.
George Wilkins.
James Fleming.
William Fleming.
Sarah Thompson.
Robert Wilson.
Peter Fleming.
James Fleming, Sr.
John Fleming.
John Kincaid.
Samuel Kincaid.
Benjamin Wales.
Samuel M'Clelland.
Charles Eaches.
William Morsel.
Robert McPherson.
John McPherson.
John Shaw.
Francis Alexander.
Walter Gilkie.

Robert Kincaid (carpenter).
Arthur Patterson.
Robert Gilkie.
Robert Kincaid (weaver).
James Keys.
Richard Hope.
Adam Hope (weaver).
Alexander Rogers.
Robert Kelly.
George Campbell.
John Miller, Esq.
John Miller, Sr.
Archibald Gay.
Joseph Wilson.
William Marshall.
John Turner.
Samuel Moore.
John Maxwell.
James Adaire.
John Irwin.
John Kincaid, Jr.
James Davidson.
James Heathrington.
David Cowan.

The above subscription was made when the Congregation at Octoraro agreed to take two-thirds of Mr. Boyd's time.

F.

EXTRACT FROM THE MINUTES OF THE SYNOD OF NEW BRUNSWICK.

MAIDENHEAD,* May 18th, 1748.

A call was brought into the Synod to be presented to the Rev. Mr. Dean from Timber Ridge and Forks of James River, the Synod refer the consideration thereof to the Presbytery of New Castle to which Mr. Dean doth belong, and do recommend it to said Presbytery to meet in Mr. Dean's meeting-house on Wednesday next upon said affair, and that Mr. Dean and his people be speedily apprised of it.†

G.

September 18th 1760

MR. CARMICHAEL.

DEAR S^r, Circumstances of Brandywine Again Oblidge us to Renew our Adress. Sr. we have the pleasure to Inform You that your one Visit has been Remarkably Blessd for the Uniting this people. Each person upon All Occasions Expressing their warmest Sentiments & Close Attachmt & Looks upon You as the only Gentleman that has preached in this place soe Every way Adapted to its Sittuation & are Morally Assured that your taking the pastoral Charge of this people wile Under Divine providence have the Most Effectual Tendency to Remove all our Distractions & perhaps be one of the Most Able & flourishing Congregations Belonging to our Synad and if Settlemt as a Vacent people is Attended with some particular Advantages & that few others in the Same Sittuation Can pretend to Viz it Ly^s Near the Seat of the Synad as wele as the Bosom of ye Prsb^r where You wile have a near Access & Correspondence with your Bretherin upon Every Emergency and has Been Ever Reputed one of the Most Healthy places As it is high Land & fule of good springs it is a Compact Congregation & few of Different Denominations Intermixed

---

* Now Lawrenceville, New Jersey.

† The Will of Mr. Dean is on record. It is a plain, well-written document, and remarkably free from the irrelevant verbiage so common at that time in legal documents.

You wile have but one people & one Meeting house & from a Long Acquaintence We are Morally Assurd You wile find a Loving Kind people that will Certainly be a pleasure to you and wile Exert the influence to Render you Comfortable & if Distressing Circumstances wile be admitted a place of Argumt where is the Vacency but Brandywine wile Turn the Scale we have Been an Orderly Congregated people Near Thirty year & for Near Twenty a Body of us has Been a Destitute people Except three years that Mr. Dean Laboured Amongst us & Now has Been Twelve Years Vacent we have made Many Attempts for the Settlemt of a Minister which proved Abortive Which Influenced Some to Leave the place Discouraged & a general Indifference took place Even in the Midst of all those Distresses or Case was Not soe peculiarly Dangerous an now by Reason of the Cececder's Unwearied Industry to propigate their Scheme & Make a party which in Some Measure they have Effected and some has said that if we Cannot obtain your Settlemt Necessity wile oblidge them to Joyne the Cececders & if this is the Case Brandywine has Done and we May only sit Down & Lament over the Ruins of the Congregation & Seeing the house of God turned to a Draught house & our Children left to Rove A Number of Meer Scepticks without any Regard to God or Religion A Dismel Reflection but Likely to be the Case if Mr Carmichael Shuts his ears to the Crye Throw Brandywine off as a Vessale of Distruction unless God Interposes in a way we know Not Now Dr Sr we wo^d Unitedly Renew our Application to you in the Language of Ruth to Naomi Intreat us not to Leave you nor from following after you in Earnest Entreaties to take the pastoral Charge of our Souls & our Children. May You be soe imprest with the Justice of our Needy Case soe as to determine your Settlemt hear & May God preside over the whole that his Glory May be advanced & his young Sern^n Made to Rejoice in Seeing the pleasure of the Lord prosper in his hand   May God be Ever at your right hand to Aid You in Every Attempt for his Glory & Beggs Leave to subscribe Yours Affectionately

    SAMLL. ALLEN FRANCIS ALEXANDER
    THOS. BROWN   FRANCIS GARDNER
    JOHN CULBERTSON WILLIAM DENNY
    WM. BROWN   WILLIAM IRWIN
    DAVID DENNY   *Ruleing Elders*

II.

JNO. CARMICHAEL'S WILL.

In the name of God, Amen. I Jno. Carmichael, of this Township of East Caln, in this County of Chester, of this State of Pennsylvania, Clergyman, being Weak in Body, & very sickly, but in the proper exercise of my reason, and realizing my mortality, that it is appointed for all Men once to die: Do make this my last Will & Testament, in manner as followeth, (viz') After committing my Soul to God who gave it, in hope of the pardon of all my Sins, and a gracious acceptance of it, through the merits, mediation, and imputted Righteousness of the Lord Jesus Christ, my dear and Blessed Saviour: And my Body to the Grave, to be interred as my surviving friends shall see proper, in a decent manner, without any needless parade or vain show whatever, as I die in the Hope of a Blessed Resurrection to eternal Life for this my mortal Body in God's good time and way, according to the Articles of the Christian Religion, as professed by the Calvinists in these latter ages in the general, but by the Presbyterian Divines in particular, whose system of Principles as expressed in our Confession of Faith & Catechisms, shorter & larger, made at Westminster, in England, by the Assembly of Divines appointed for that purpose, and have been and now is, adopted by the Synod of New York and Philadelphia, in America, I give my Testimony to, on this my Death Bed, as expressive of the mind & will of God, contained in the Holy Scriptures, with the exceptions the aforesaid Synod have ordinarily made, but more especially & particularly, do I desire to give my Death Bed Testimony, to the necessity of an experimental knowledge of those Doctrines, contained in the aforesaid Systems, called the Doctrines of Grace, to be applied to and impressed on the soul by the Holy Ghost, in a saving manner, to Prepare the soul for that eternal felicity which consists in the enjoyment of God in Heaven. But as to the few things of this Life or Worldly Substance with which God has blessed me, I Will to have them disposed of, for the good of my surviving Family, my Widow and Children, in the following manner:—I Will that that piece of Land which was Run out & measured by Thomas Haslet the survayer last Spring, which contains near One Hundred

Acres of Land & lies on the East side of this Plantation, joining the Land & Lines of William Wilson, Adam Guthery, William Headings & Widow Rachel White, be sold to the highest bidder and a good authentick tittle made to the purchaser by my Executors hereafter mentioned: and the Money that arises from the Sale of said Land, to be divided into three equal parts; one third part to my Oldest Son John Flavel Carmichael, as soon as the money can be got, the other third part to Washington Gates Carmichael, my second son, to help him in Education, and to be in the hands of his mother or Guardian for that purpose, as I desire this son may receive a good Education, fit for the Gospel Ministry, if he has a turn for it, And the other third part to be given to my oldest daughter, Phebe, when she comes to the Age of Twenty two years, to be hers forever. As to the rest of this Plantation, which contains the most valuable part of the improvements, such as the House, Garden, meadows, Barn & Orchard &c" my will is, that the premisses be apprized, together with all & singular the goods & Chattels of every kind; and then a just estimate taken of the whole, and one whole third part thereof to belong to my dear and loving Wife, then a Widow, to be hers forever, which I will & appoint to her, in lieu of the whole of all her dower, be the same more or less. My Will further is, that the other two thirds of the whole apprized Estate, be divided equally among my Six Children, John Flavel, Phebe, Catherine Mustard, Washington Gates, Elizabeth Sarah, & Francina, Share & Share alike, be the same more or less, each child to receive his Share when come to the Age of Twenty one years; the mother is to receive the benefit of the profits of the Minor Children's Shares, while they continue to live with her & no longer, whether her own or her Step Children. Also my Will is, that if any of my Children to whom I have thus divided my Estate, depart this Life before he or she comes to legal Age, to heir his or her portion, his or her Share be equally devided among the surviving Children, Share & Share alike. Also my Will is, that if my Widow and the Executors shall conclude & judge, that it will be better for the Widow & Children to sell these premises or plantation, and to move to some place such as Princeton, where the Education of the Children can be more easily assertained, or whereever they shall judge proper, in such case, let the place be sold to the best Advantage; and may the kind good providence of the God of Abraham, Isaac & Jacob direct them. I do hereby appoint, & ordain & constitute, my very trusty dear & worthy friends to be Executors of this my last Will & Testament, (viz.) the Hon: William Clingan Esqr, the Hon^{bl} John Beaton Esqr, together with my Son John Flavel Carmichael, hereby declaring this to be my last Will & Testament, and hereby cancelling and *disanulling* all preceding ones as null and void. In Witness whereof, I have hereunto set my Hand & Seal, this 17th day of August, One Thousand Seven Hundred & Eighty-five.

JOHN CARMICHAEL [Seal]

GEORGE IRWIN,
BARNABAS CURLY his V Mark
   Witnesses.

I, John Carmichael within named, continuing Weak & Sick in Body, but through the divine goodness, of sound disposing mind & Memory, do think proper to make this Codicil, or Addition to my last Will and Testament, in the manner following, vizt Whereas, I have certain sums of money in the Fund of the Corporation for the relief of Presbyterian Ministers their Widows & Children, which by the Rules of the said Corporation, will be productive of a certain Annuity or yearly allowance to my Family after my decease, Now it is my Will and I order, that all the Monies that may be drawn yearly from the said fund, be paid to my beloved Wife, to be applied towards her support, and the support Education and maintenance of my minor Children, to wit, Catherine Mustard, Washington Gates, Elizabeth Sarah & Francina, during their minority, to be apply'd to her & their use afores^d while She continues my Widow, and the said Children remain under her care and management; but in case they the said Children should be taken from under her care by their Guardian or otherwise, In that Case I will & order that the said yearly Annuity be divided between my said Wife and Children in the following manner, vizt One third thereof to my beloved Wife, and the remaining two thirds to be equally divided among my Four Children above named. I Likewise give and devise unto my Son John Flavel Carmichael, all that my One undivided moiety or equal half part of Fourteen Acres of Valuable, Woodland, situate in the Town of Newark, in the County of Essex, in New Jersey, which came to me as a part of the Dowry of his deceased Mother; to hold to him the said John Flavel Carmichael & to his Heirs & Assigns forever, I Likewise Give & bequeath unto my said son Flavel, my wearing Apparel and Cane. And I do hereby declare this Codicil to be part & parcel of my last Will and Testament, hereby ratifying & confirming the same and every part thereof. In Witness whereof, I have hereunto set my Hand & Seal, this eleventh day of November, in the year of our Lord One Thousand, Seven Hundred & Eighty-five. Before signing, & sealing, I nominate & appoint Mr. William Hunter of West Nantmeal, to be one of the Executors of my last Will & Testament.

JOHN CARMICHAEL [Seal]

Signed, Sealed, published & declared by the Testator as a Codicil to his last Will & Testament in the presence of Us

ROBERT FILSON,
GEORGE IRWIN.

I.

DR. GRIER'S RESIGNATION.

Dr. Grier's request for a dissolution of the pastoral relation was brought before Presbytery for its action April 14, 1869. It was in writing, and as follows:

To THE MODERATOR AND PRESBYTERY OF NEW CASTLE.

DEAR BRETHREN,—In the year of our Lord 1813, in the twenty-first year of my age, I was licensed by this Presbytery to preach the Gospel, and on the 24th day of November, A.D. 1814, I was ordained to the full work of the Ministry, and installed Pastor of the Congregation of the Forks of the Brandywine.

Now, in the seventy-sixth year of my age, and having labored amongst you for fifty-four years and seven months, and paralyzed both in my speech and limbs, and no longer able to fulfil the duties of the Pastorate, I ask this Presbytery, not one of whom was a member of it when I was ordained and installed, to dissolve the pastoral relation existing now between me and the Congregation of the Forks of Brandywine.

J. N. C. GRIER.

March 30, 1869.

At a meeting of the Presbytery of Newcastle, held May 6, 1869, the subjoined resolutions were presented by the Rev. John M. Dickey, D.D., and adopted:

Resolved, That in accepting the resignation of Dr. J. N. C. Grier of his charge of the Brandywine Manor Church, the Presbytery of New Castle desire to express their grateful acknowledgment of God's goodness and mercy in permitting this pastoral relation to continue so long; reaching over more than fifty-four years, marked by many precious seasons of special religious interest, and by a continual ingathering of souls, the Presbytery would note the fact; and now as growing infirmity renders it necessary that Dr. Grier be released from his charge, they offer him their heartfelt sympathy, and pray that the joys of a faithful minister may, through the merits of our Lord and Saviour, be his now and in the church above.

Resolved, That the above be entered on the minutes, and that a copy be handed to the Elder of Brandywine Manor Church, to be presented to Dr. Grier.

J.
CONSTITUTION OF THE HONEYBROOK TEMPERANCE SOCIETY.

The undersigned, inhabitants of Honeybrook and its vicinity, impressed with a sense of the incalculable injury resulting to society, in all its present and eternal interests, from the existence and prevalence of Intemperance, in the use of intoxicating liquors, feel themselves called upon as good citizens to make all the efforts within their ability, by fair and honorable means, to lessen and if possible to extirpate the vice. And for this purpose do associate together, under a pledge of mutual co-operation, according to the provisions of the following articles, viz.:

I. To abstain from all use of intoxicating liquors, excepting when we conscientiously believe they are necessary as a medicine.

II. To refrain from offering them to our friends and visitors, in our families, as marks of hospitality.

III. Entirely to cease giving them to workmen and laborers, in harvest or any other season, excepting as above specified.

IV. To refrain under the strictest caution from selling, or giving them in greater or smaller quantities to persons known to be in the habit of making a bad use of them, except when known to be needed as medicine.

V. That we will neither sell nor cause to be sold any of our grain for the purpose of distillation.

VI. That we will hold the vice of intemperance in utter abhorrence, and use every proper means to bring it into the disrepute and destruction due to its hatefulness, and yet regarding its victims and its advocates with deep compassion, and to use all our efforts to reclaim them.

Any person making application, and being at the time sober, may become a member of this association; and any person known to the society to have violated any of these articles shall be conversed with on the subject, and for a repetition of the offence shall be dismissed.

John N. C. Grier,	John Clemenson,
Samuel Jones,	John Buchanan,
John W. Pinkerton,	William Ewing,
John Ballentine,	James K. Mendenhall,
C. Robinson,	James Quin,
Thomas G. Happersett,	John Wright,
David Skeen,	Nathan Griffith,
James M'Clune,	Benj. Talbot,
Joseph Brown,	Joseph Criley,
John Stewart,	Joseph Whitaker,
Wm. Templeton,	Geo. Cowan,
James Ralston,	David Buchanan, Jr.
James Ralston, Jr.	Wm. Robeson.*

K.

COPY OF DEED FOR THE LAND FIRST OBTAINED FOR CHURCH PURPOSES.

This Indenture, made the eighteenth day of May in the year of our Lord one thousand seven hundred and sixty-one, between Matthew

---

* The only survivors are Mr. Ballentine and he who records the fact.

Robertson, of West Nantmel and John Smith the younger of East Caln in the County of Chester and province of Pennsylvania, Yeomen of the one part and The Reverend John Carmichael, Clerk, John Culbertson, James Moore, William Denny, Samuel McKinley, and Francis Gardner, all of the said County of Chester, Yeomen of the other part. Whereas the Honorable The proprietaries of the said province by their Letter Patent the fifth day of this Instant, May, did grant and confirm unto The said Matthew Robertson and John Smith in Fee, A certain piece of Land situated in their Manor of Springton in the said County of Chester, and Township of Westnantmell, Beginning at a post in the Line of the Manor afore'd Corner of the tract of land part of the said manor surveyed unto James McCoskry thence by said McCoskry's land and along the great road leading through the said Manor from Philada. to Harris's Ferry on the River Susquehannah called Paxtang Road North fifty five degrees, East fifty perches to a post and South fifty one degrees, East forty six perches to a post in the Manor Line—thence along the Manor Line, west seventy seven perches to the Place of Beginning, containing six acres and eighty six perches with the appurtenances (except as therein excepted) To hold to the said Matthew Robertson and John Smith their Heirs and Assigns forever, to and for the Use of Intent and Purpose of erecting and continuing thereon a Church or House of Religious Worship for the use of the said Congregation of Presbyterians and their Descendents and Successors for ever, in such Manner as the Minister, Elders, and majority of such Congregation for the Time being shall from Time to Time order, direct and appoint, under the yearly Quit Rent of one Shilling Sterling Money of Great Britain to the said proprietaries their Heirs and Successors for ever as in and by the said recited patent record at Philadelphia in Patent Book A.A. vol. 2, pa. 285, more fully appears. Now this Indenture witnesseth that the said Matthew Robertson and John Smith at the special instance and Request of the said Presbyterian Congregation and by and with the Privity, Consent, Approbation and Direction of them or the major part of them who now statedly worship in the Church or Meeting House erected on the said described and granted piece of Land under the pastoral Charge of the Reverend the said John Carmichael, testified by his and the rest of the said parties hereto of the Second Part being the Trustees chosen and appointed by the said Congregation for that purpose signing and sealing the presents hereby acknowledge and declare that the names of the said Matthew Robertson and John Smith were made use of in the said recited Patent or Grant and the same was so as aforesaid made or intended to be made to them, the said Matthew Robertson and John Smith and their Heirs in trust only to and for the use, Benefit and Behoof of the People who are and shall be members of the said Presbyterian Congregation according to the tenor and true meaning of these presents for ever. And the said Matthew Robertson and John Smith by and with the like, consent, privity, and direction of the said Congregation or the Majority of them as aforesaid and in consideration of the sum of five shillings apiece to them in hand paid by the said parties hereto of the second part (the receipt thereof, is hereby acknowledged) have granted, bargained, sold, enfeoffed released and confirmed and by these presents, do grant, bargain, sell, enfeoff release and confirm unto the said John Carmichael, John Culbertson, James Moore, William Denny, Samuel McKinley, Francis Gardner and their Heirs and Assigns, All that the said herein before described piece or parcel of land containing six acres and eighty six perches of land be the same more or less, together with all the buildings, improvements rights members, and appurtenances thereto belonging and the reversions and remainders thereof, and the said sealed Patent *to have and to hold* the said described six acres and eighty six perches piece or portion of ground Hereditaments and premises hereby granted or mentioned or intended so to be with the appurtenances unto the said John Carmichael, John Culbertson, James Moore, William Denny, Francis Gardner, and Samuel McKinley their Heirs and Assigns forever In Trust and of intent and purpose that the said described and granted piece of land shall be and continue a place for the site of a House of Public Worship and for a burial place, and that the whole of the said premises shall be, continue, and remain for the use and service of the said congregation of people called Presbyterians forever, who do or shall hold and continue to hold the system of Doctrine contained in the Westminster Confession of Faith and Directory agreeable to the present Interpretation of the Synod of New York and Philadelphia to which they are now united, but under and subject nevertheless to the following conditions and limitations viz.: Provided always that no person shall be deemed to belong to the said Congregation until he has statedly attended upon the Public Worship of God in the said Congregation for the space of twelve months and shall have regularly contributed to the support of the ministry and other charges of the same according to the usage of Presbyterians, nor shall be deemed any longer a member thereof than he continues to hold and conform to the Westminster Confession of Faith and Directory aforesaid, and shall continue to attend statedly in an orderly manner upon the public Worship of God in the said Congregation and be in Communion with the said Synod as before expressed. And provided also that neither the said parties hereto of the Second Part nor either of them nor any other person or persons succeeding them in this Trust who shall hereafter fall from or change his or their religious Principles aforesaid or separate from the said Synod or depart from the said Congregation, or who shall refuse or neglect to contribute toward the support of the same, shall be capable to execute this Trust or stand secured to the Uses aforesaid nor have any right or interest in the said described or granted piece of land and premises or in the House or other buildings and improvements thereon erected or to be erected as aforesaid while he or they shall so continue but that in such cases as also when any of them or other person or persons who shall succeed in the Trust aforesaid shall happen to depart this Life that then it shall and may be lawful for the said congregation the time being and from time to time and as often as the occasion shall require to make choice of others to manage the said Trust instead of such that as shall fall away, secede, separate or be deceased. Provided further, in order to prevent law suits in case it shall be disputed in time coming whether any particular persons or members of the said Congregation or any debate shall arise in relation to Pews in the said House of Worship that all such debates and all others of a civil nature respecting the said Tract of Land and House of Worship shall be finally determined by a majority of votes of the adult male members of the said congregation being such afore convened after Public Notice in which Public Conventions, the minister of the said Congregation for the time being if present, shall always preside as Moderator or by Arbitrators holding the Principles aforesaid chosen by them for the purpose aforesaid. And the said Matthew Robertson and John Smith or either of them do further acknowledge and declare by these presents that they neither claim nor have by virtue of the said Patent or Grant to them any right, Title or Interest in the said described and granted piece or portion of Ground and premises or any part thereof, their own particular order and benefit but only to and for the Trust, Uses, Purposes and Services herein before mentioned and to no other use and service whatsoever and therefore in further accomplishment and performance of the Trust and Confidence aforesaid, they the said Matthew Robertson and John Smith do for themselves and every of them and for each of their heirs severally and respectively warrant, promise, grant, and agree to and with the said parties hereto of the Second Part their heirs, executors, Assigns and every of them by these presents that they the said Matthew Robertson, and John Smith their Heir and Assigns shall and will at all or any time or times hereafter upon the request of the said congregation or a majority of the male members thereof convened as aforesaid make, do execute and acknowledge all such further and other act and Acts conveyance and assurance whatsoever in the Law as shall be advised by Council learned in the Law to be needful for the better conveying and vesting the said premises in the Succeeding Trust and further assuming of the said described Tract or piece of Land with the appurtenances to and for the Uses, Interests, and Purposes aforesaid. In witness thereof the parties aforesaid to these presents have hereunto interchangeably set their hands and seals the day and year first above Written.

    WM. DENNY   MATTHEW ROBERTSON
    SAMUEL MCKINLEY JOHN SMITH
    FRANS. GARDNER JOHN CULBERTSON
    JOHN CARMICHAEL JAMES MOORE.

Sealed and Delivered
 SAMUEL ALLEN
 JAMES MCCOSKRY
 ROBERT SMITH

Chester ss

Before me William Clingan one of the Justices for said County came the above named Matthew Robertson and John Smith, the above grantors who did acknowledge the above Instrument of Writing to be their Act and Deed by them signed, sealed and delivered for the uses and purposes above mentioned.

Acknowledged Decr 21st 1761
            WILLIAM CLINGAN.

L.

INSTRUCTORS IN HOWARD ACADEMY.

Principals.	Assistants in Young Men's Department.	In Young Ladies' Department.
James M'Clune, LL.D.	Mr. Isaac M'Dermond.	Miss Gwenny Rowland.
Rev. Mr. Ogden.	" John C. Thompson.	" Elizabeth Sims.
Rev. Mr. Kirkland.	" Samuel R. Forrest.	" Alice Hotchkins.
Mr. Watson.	" John K. Ralston.	" Louisa B. Ralston.
	" James B. Ralston.	" Marion Thibeaudeaux.*

M.

REV. JAMES GRIER.

The Rev. James Grier was born in Bucks County, Pa., about 1750. Where he received his academical training is not known. He was graduated at the head of his class by the College of New Jersey in 1772, and passed a year as a tutor in that institution. He was hopefully converted by the preaching of Whitefield, and studied theology under the direction of Dr. Witherspoon.

Mr. Grier was licensed by the Presbytery of Philadelphia in 1775, and installed as pastor of Deep Run Presbyterian Church, Bucks County, Pa., in 1778, where he remained until his death. He preached his last sermon November 18, 1791, and died the next day.

Mr. Grier was an excellent scholar, a faithful and instructive minister of the Gospel. His only son, John Ferguson Grier, organized and became pastor of the first Presbyterian Church in Reading, Pennsylvania.

Although fully competent both by learning and ability to prepare works worthy of remembrance, Mr. Grier, like nearly all of the Presbyterian clergymen of his day in the Middle States, gave no production of his pen to the public. This is the more remarkable as the press of New England, during the last century, especially, teemed with Thanksgiving Sermons, Funeral Orations, Patriotic Addresses and less ephemeral productions.†

---

* Records of Howard Academy; Reminiscences of First Principal.

† Sprague, "Annals of American Pulpit;" Dr. S. Alexander, "Princeton College in the Eighteenth Century;" Elliot, "Biographical Dictionary."

N.

BRANDYWINE CREEK.

This stream, the Susquehanna of Chester County, retains the name given it by the Dutch, while they held possession of the country around its outlet. Brandywein Kill, clear-water river, is mentioned by the First Governor under the Duke of York in 1665. On account of the abundance of fish in its waters this stream was much frequented by the Indians, and its banks were among their favorite camping-grounds. Many of the sites for propelling machinery afforded by its rapid current were utilized at an early period. Several of the first grist-mills erected West of the Delaware River were dependent on this water-course for their motive-power.

Owing to the clearing away of the forests, giving rise to greater evaporation, and the removal of fallen timber and other obstructions from its channel, permitting the rain-fall to pass off more rapidly, this stream is much smaller than it was a century ago. A ferry was kept several years by Chadd at the crossing which bears his name, and when the Hessians attempted to force a passage at that place during the ill-starred battle fought on its banks, they were obliged to carry their muskets on a level with the shoulder, and many of the wounded by Wayne's artillery were drowned.

There are few streams of no greater length nor volume of water more noteworthy than the Brandywine. This is manifest whether attention is directed to the conflict which bears its name, the numerous factories for which it supplies the motive-power, or the well-tilled farms of the moral and intelligent communities which people the large portion of Chester County which it drains.

The Presbyterians indicated the locality of their first Meeting-Houses and the religious associations connected with them by giving them the names of the nearest known natural objects, as streams, valleys, levels, etc. Thus Great Valley, Neshaminy, Deep Run, Head of Christiana, Octoraro, Doe Run, Chestnut Level, and Forks of Brandywine, or in the quaint style and orthography of Adam Boyd, the Fforks.

The Friends rejecting the Indian names as savoring of heathenism, called their houses for public worship after the Townships in which they were placed, as Birmingham, Goshen, Uwchlan, Nantmeal, Caln, etc. That they did so is a matter for regret, as it has caused the original names of nearly all the streams in Chester County to be forgotten. In Lancaster, Berks, and other Counties a majority of the water-courses retain, with some modifications, the names they received from the Aborigines, but in Chester County two streams only, the Pocopson and Octoraro, perpetuate the remembrance of the most friendly and unwarlike of the Indian tribes.

While the annals of many portions of this State contain details of "Indian outrages," the history of one of the oldest Counties shows that the Lenni Lenape and their "white brothers" dwelt peaceably together along the Brandywine and other streams upwards of a hundred years.*

O.

NANTMELL TOWNSHIP.

This Township, now divided into five, was formed and some settlements made along its Western limit by Welsh immigrants in 1720-22. It included a large area, being bounded on the North by French Creek, West by the mountain (Welsh Mountain), Southeast by the Barren Hill, and Northeast in part by Marsh Creek. When Lancaster County was set off from Chester, in 1729, the division line between the two Counties became the Western limit of Nantmell, while the Southeast boundary of Springtown Manor, laid out in the same year, separated it from Caln.

Nantmell remained almost an unsettled wilderness until the Scotch Irish, who landed at Newcastle in 1729, and the years immediately following, passing up the Brandywine and along the "Indian Trail" which led from the Great Valley to Conestogo Valley, chose this township as their places of abode.

The Scotch and Scotch-Irish were the poorest in worldly goods and the least refined of the first settlers, but being energetic, economical, and industrious, they soon dotted the Township with humble but

* Smith, "History of Delaware County;" Day, "Historical Collections;" "Hazard's Register of Pennsylvania."

APPENDIX.   257

comfortable homes. As they, like all who came to America at that period, sought "freedom to worship God" rather than wealth, a church was soon organized and a building for public worship provided. The Manor Meeting-House, the first in Nantmell Township, and for a hundred years the only Presbyterian Church within its boundaries, was built in less than three years after records prove that those who erected it had become settled residents.

The first dwellings were made of unhewn logs; the barns were small and thatched with straw. The buildings were placed near a spring, no wells having been sunk until at least half a century afterwards, and the now common suction-pump unknown till upward of thirty years later. Coming from countries where timber was scarce and valuable, and not being skilled in wielding the axe, they spared the forests, making ditches the boundaries of farms, and using the privet for the separation of fields.

The section of country included in Nantmell being elevated, and the currents in the streams rapid, the purity and abundance of the water, an object of particular interest with the first settlers, caused it to be named and settled sooner than many other portions of the County. As further evidence of this, it may be stated that the name of the Township, Nantmell, or good water, of the principal stream, Brandywine Kill, clear-water river, and Springtown, the name of the Manor, all refer to the water, and what is worthy of remark, each of these names was given by immigrants of different nationalities. Nantmell by the Welsh, Brandywein by the Dutch, and Springtown by the English.

The Indians appear to have appreciated the advantages of the bracing air, pure water, and abundance of fish and game which Nantmell afforded, as one of their principal towns and burial-places was situated in this Township.

The influence of the Manor Church, which, after the lapse of one hundred and fifty years, still flourishes, is manifest both in the general morality of the inhabitants and in the fact that *eight* out of every *ten* of those who own the farms occupied by their forefathers are descendants of members of that church.

Although Nantmell has produced few literary or scientific men, yet two natives of it have received the degree of D.D., two of LL.D., and at least four members of the Chester County bar, three editors of ably-conducted periodicals, nine physicians and two well-known educators claim Nantmell as the home of their infancy.*

P.

As evidence of the sparse population at that period, the following list of those who settled between 1720 and 1740 in that part of Caln now included in East and West Brandywine, is given:

Edwin Irwin.	Joshua Mendenhall.
Joseph Eldridge.	James McFarlane.
Robert Mirach.	William Litore.
John McDermond.	Andrew Elliott.
Samuel M'Crary.	John Green.
Thomas Green.	John Byers.
John Patterson.	James McGlaughlin.
Andrew Cox.	John McFarlan.
James Green.	Adam Guthrie.
James Love.	Francis Long.
William Patterson.	Joseph Wilkinson.
John Troak.	James Batten.
William Smart.	Richard Buffington.
Samuel McKinly.	William Byers.
Henry Lewis.	Samuel Byers.
Peter Whitaker.	Joseph Phipps.
William Reese.	Henry Jones.
Patrick Lockhart.	George Oglesby.
John Morgan.	John Walker.
Thomas Temple.	Peter Graham.

In 1722 there were but eight thousand inhabitants in what was then Chester County; that is, all of Pennsylvania except the Counties of Bucks and Philadelphia.

* Local Memoranda; Colonial Records.

Q.

EXTRACT FROM MINUTES OF PRESBYTERY.
SEPTEMBER, 1716.

Meetings or Presbyteries constituting one annually as a synod, to meet at Philadelphia or elsewhere, to consist of all the members of each subordinate Presbytery or meeting for this year at least. Therefore, it is agreed by the Presbytery after serious deliberation, that the first subordinate meeting or Presbytery do meet at Philadelphia, or elsewhere, as they shall see fit, to consist of these, viz., Messrs. Andrews, Jones, Powell, Orr, Pradner, and Morgan, and the second to meet at New Castle, or elsewhere, as they shall see fit, to consist of these, viz., Messrs. Anderson, Magill, Gillespie, Wotherspoon, Evans, and Conn. The third to meet at Snowhill, or elsewhere, to consist of these, viz., Messrs. Davies, Hampton, and Henry.

Of the above Fifteen Presbyterian Clergymen, only one, Andrews, was a native. All of the others were immigrants from Scotland, Ireland, or Wales.

R.

LIST OF THOSE BURIED IN THE GRAVEYARDS FROM MARCH, 1849, TO APRIL, 1863, FOURTEEN YEARS.

Name.	Date of Burial.	Name.	Date of Burial.
Arthur Donegan,	April 25, 1849.	Alexander Maitland,	Nov. 13, 1849.
George W. Nelson,	May 1, "	John C. Thompson,	Dec. 9, "
William H. Lockart,	" 9, "	Joseph Arters,	Jan. 13, 1850.
Jacob Happersett,	June 15, "	Child of J. Sheneman,	" 26, "
Margaret Conaway,	July 31, "	" of Charles M'Cann,	Feb. 11, "
Robert Caruthers,	Aug. 2, "	Sarah S. Sides,	" 12, "
Mary Donegan,	" 9, "	Jane H. Grier,	Mar. 1, "
Richard Donegan,	" 16, "	Child of David Bunn,	" 24, "
Child of Walter Lilly,	" 26, "	Ann Robinson,	April 11, "
William Templeton, Sr.,	Sept. 2, "	Robert Brice,	" 29, "
Margaret Donegan,	" 6, "	Esther Smith,	May 2, "
Letitia Lewis,	" 24, "	Magdalina Shultz,	June 16, "
Child of John Grier,	" 26, "	Susanna S. Torbet,	July 9, "
Caroline Lapp,	Oct. 3, "	Child of Wm. Guthrie,	" 16, "
Ann Maris,	" 28, "	Rachel Guthrie,	" 30, "
Susan Haup,	Nov. 3, "	Grenabaum Jews,	Aug. 7, "

APPENDIX.

Name.	Date of Burial.	Name.	Date of Burial.
Child of James Long,	Aug. 8, 1850.	Elizabeth Carpenter,	Mar. 31, 1852.
Josiah P. Dowlin,	" 10, "	Evan Granger,	April 5, "
Elizabeth McIntyre,	" 24, "	Child of Robert Dorlan,	May 1, "
Theodore S. Torbert,	Sept. 27, "	Mrs. Robert Dowlin,	" 9, "
Jesse Lockhart,	" 27, "	Child of Jas. Millegan,	July 2, "
Jane Erwin,	Oct. 9, "	Andrew Morton,	" 21, "
Elizabeth Elliott,	Nov. 8, "	John Dowlin,	Aug. 3, "
Child of John Bradly,	" 14, "	Elizabeth Gibson,	" 9, "
Elizabeth D. Dorlan,	" 22, "	Jane Marshall,	" 13, "
Daniel Campbell,	Dec. 6, "	Sarah Rigg,	" 20, "
Rachel Happersett,	" 13, "	Margaret Milnes,	Sept. 9, "
Margaret Bunn,	" 19, "	Hannah Johnson,	" 13, "
Child of M. Osborn,	" 23, "	E. Ralston,	Oct. 8, "
Alice Long,	Jan. 9, 1851.	Martha McAdams,	" 31. "
John Umstead,	" 11, "	Child of Wm. Watson,	Nov. 5, "
Jacob Umstead,	" 11, "	Child of Ezekiel Rigg,	Dec. 5, "
Child of Robert Neely,	" 11, "	Sarah Davis,	Jan. 9, 1853.
Hannah Freeman,	Feb. 10, "	Nathan Dorlan,	Feb. 15, "
Sarah Dorlan,	" 9, "	Child of Walter Lilly,	Mar. 15, "
Soloman A. Smith,	" 11, "	Mary Ann Clour,	" 20, "
Robert Kerr,	" 26, "	Ester Torbitt,	" 22, "
Elizabeth Buchanan,	Mar. 4, "	Milo Gibbony,	" 31, "
Elizabeth Swinchart,	June 2, "	John K. Clour,	April 7, "
Child of Robt. Dowlin,	July 19, "	William Allan,	" 16, "
" " "	" 26, "	Child of B. Baldwin,	" 19, "
Child of R. Smith,	Aug. 5, "	Child of K. Clour,	May 9, "
Sarah J. McKim,	" 7, "	Martha White,	" 11, "
Child of Jas. Millegan,	Sept. 5, "	Sarah Freeman,	" 13, "
Clarrissa Marple,	" 18, "	A. Child,	" 22, "
Isabella Criley,	" 21, "	Elizabeth Allen,	June 23, "
Caroline Happersett,	" 26, "	Matthew A. Stanly,	July 1, "
Mary J. Neely,	" 30, "	Caleb Pusey,	" 10, "
Joseph Hughes,	Oct. 12, "	Robert McWilliams,	" 15, "
Jane Shafer,	" 24, "	Catharine Grier,	Aug. 4, "
Child of James Way,	" 27, "	Child of D. West,	" 6, "
Thomas Dorlan,	Nov. 10, "	Joanna Bones,	" 25, "
Susannah Stanly,	" 21, "	John Hood,	" 31, "
Samuel Lewis,	" 22, "	Child of J. Dauman,	Sept. 14, "
William Jackson,	" 25, "	Child of Alex. Maitland,	Oct. 3, "
Parmenas Crowe,	Dec. 6, "	Samuel S. Barford,	" 10, "
David Lockhart,	Jan. 31, 1852.	Hannah Stanly,	" 11, "
John Arters,	Feb. 6, "	Mrs. Buffington,	" 18, "
Child of John Shingle,	" 17, "	Isaac McGlaughlin,	Nov. 17, "
John H. Long,	Mar. 1, "	Child of T. Matlack,	" 18, "
Joseph Dorlan,	" 2, "	Samuel Barnet,	" 25, "
Henry Sheneman,	" 5, "	Joseph Rhea,	Dec. 16, "
Walter B. Lilly,	" 27, "	Child of J. Gibbony,	Jan. 9, 1854.

APPENDIX. 261

Name.	Date of Burial.	Name.	Date of Burial.
Grier Russell,	Feb. 3, 1854.	Francis Harris,	Dec. 20, 1855.
Rachel McGlaughlin,	" 7, "	Emma Mackelduff,	Jan. 2, 1856.
Jane Parke,	" 18, "	Dorothea Vastine,	" 3, "
M. Guincy,	" 23, "	Hannah Kennedy,	" 9, "
Phœbe Kerns,	Mar. 6, "	M. Strong,	Feb. 8, "
Child of T. Sellers,	" 20, "	Mary Dorlan,	" 15, "
Sarah Lewis,	April 3, "	Jane Caruthers,	" 28, "
Rebecca Happersett,	" 6, "	William Hunter,	April 4, "
Elizabeth Clour,	" 9, "	J. Hammond,	" 9, "
Maria Marshall,	" 12, "	Mary J. Walkinshaw,	" 10, "
Hannah Granger,	" 17, "	Child of R. Walkinshaw,	" 12, "
Keziah Umstead,	May 4, "	Child of L. Hammond,	" 15, "
Child of S. Dorlan,	" 9, "	Jane Moore,	June 7, "
Mary Smith,	" 10, "	Elizabeth McClellan,	" 14, "
Thomas M'Clune,	" 13, "	John Forbis,	" 15, "
Martha Mackelduff,	June 13, "	Agnes Thompson,	" 29, "
Barbara Griffith,	" 25, "	Joseph Rhea,	July 23, "
Jane Neely,	July 8, "	George Floyd,	Aug. 7, "
Elizabeth Essick,	" 9, "	James Williams,	Sept. 2, "
Harman Smith,	" 27, "	Elizabeth Ballentine,	" 26, "
Mary Smith,	Aug. 3, "	Child of L. Hammond,	Oct. 2, "
Harner Umstead,	Sept. 26, "	Josiah Brower,	" 4, "
Harriet Dowlin,	" 26, "	John Sloan,	Nov. 8, "
Archibald Campbell,	" 30, "	Child of C. Maffett,	" 12, "
Emma M. Martin,	Oct. 1, "	Melchi Happersett,	" 22, "
Isaac Lewis,	" 3, "	Lavinia Maitland,	" 29, "
Child of Wm. Dowlin,	" 5, "	Sarah Boyce,	Dec. 3, "
Jonathan Benner,	" 14. "	Susan Lilly,	" 28, "
Child of Wm. Dowlin,	" 17, "	Child of J. Sterrett,	Jan. 11, 1857.
Child of James Neely,	Nov. 2, "	Mary Wilson,	" 26, "
Sarah Aikins,	Dec. 7, "	Child of H. Swinehart,	" 27, "
Samuel Pergrin,	Jan. 9, 1855.	Rebecca Grier,	Feb. 14, "
Joseph Martin, Jr.,	" 18, "	Sarah Brown,	" 23, "
Nancy Pinkerton,	Mar. 4, "	James W. Brown,	Mar. 11, "
Jane Freeman,	" 23, "	Samuel Caruthers,	" 15, "
Esther Long,	April 11, "	Child of A. Martin,	" 29, "
Isabella Divine,	" 15, "	Child of Clark Guincy,	April 10, "
Child of Jno. Dauman,	July 11, "	Joseph Martin,	" 25, "
Rebecca Graham,	" 18, "	Joseph Kerr,	May 10, "
Child of Wm. Loag,	" 21, "	Child of R. Mason,	" 17, "
Elizabeth Dorlan,	Aug. 11, "	David Lockhart,	" 24, "
Jane A. Galligher,	" 25, "	John Kurtz,	June 6, "
Child of J. McCurdy,	Sept. 4, "	Benjamin Harris,	" 7, "
Ann Forbis,	" 16, "	Child of J. Williams,	" 9, "
Parke Moore,	Nov. 3, "	James H. Long,	July 14, "
Joseph Britton,	Dec. 2, "	Alexander Gavitt,	" 20, "
Child of J. Mason,	" 19, "	J. Neely,	Aug. 4, "

APPENDIX.

Name.	Date of Burial.	Name.	Date of Burial.
Samuel Dorlan,	Aug. 26, 1857.	William Dauman,	Jan. 3, 1859.
Mr. Gallagher,	Sept. 6, "	Mrs. Townsley,	Feb. 19, "
Josiah Williams,	" 8, "	Margaret Mills,	" 24, "
Nathaniel Pennington,	" 30, "	Margaret A. McKim,	Mar. 2, "
Franklin French,	Oct. 2, "	Child of S. Way,	" 4, "
John Strong,	" 13, "	Wilson Brown,	" 15, "
Charles Umstead,	Nov. 14, "	Phœbe Carmichael,	" 17, "
Jane R. Walker,	" 25, "	Isabella Osborne,	April 5, "
William Williams,	Dec. 6, "	John Fernwalt,	" 10, "
John Widener,	" 7, "	Margaret Stevenson,	" 12, "
William Roberts,	" 11, "	Mary Gibson,	" 30, "
Nathan Pinkerton,	Jan. 5, 1858.	Child of R. Serril,	May 24, "
William W. Elliott,	" 12, "	Eliza R. Thomas,	" 30, "
M. McAdams,	" 18, "	Frederick Wonderly,	" 30, "
Frances Williams,	Feb. 9, "	Jane Shineman,	June 19, "
—— Boyce,	" 11, "	Amy Marple,	" 30, "
Daniel Welsh,	" 16, "	Susannah Dorlan,	July 3, "
James Welch, Jr.,	" 18, "	Kate Hatfield,	Aug. 4, "
Samuel Culbertson,	Mar. 3, "	Mary Curry,	" 4, "
Child of J. Strong,	" 16, "	Cecilia Hatfield,	" 10, "
Nancy F. Grier,	" 22, "	Child of G. Wonderly,	" 24, "
William Arters,	" 28, "	Ruth Sterrett,	" 29, "
Miss Rhea,	" 30, "	Thomas G. Ralston,	Oct. 3, "
Child of Wm. King,	May 6, "	John Forbis,	Nov. 1, "
Nathan Dorlan,	" 6, "	Sarah McClellan,	Dec. 28, "
Jacob Darkess,	" 20, "	John Dunwoody,	Jan. 21, 1860.
J. Cain,	" 20, "	George Forbis,	" 27, "
Annie Maitland,	" 30, "	Mary Christin,	" 31, "
Joseph Williams,	June 4, "	John Umstead,	Mar. 8, "
Elizabeth Athens,	" 27, "	Martha Maitland,	" 14, "
Daniel Shuman,	July 2, "	Susan Russell,	April 23, "
Isaac Williams,	" 11, "	Mary Ballentine,	" 30, "
Child of J. McCurdy,	" 15, "	John Worrall,	May 25, "
Jane L. Grier,	" 19, "	Margaret M'Clune,	July 8, "
Child of J. Sterrett,	" 27, "	Jane Templeton,	" 17, "
John Saffer,	Aug. 1, "	Child of Chas. McCann,	" 19, "
Child of A. Ludwick,	" 16, "	Child of Clark Guiney,	" 27, "
Margaret A. Weber,	" 21, "	Margaret Arters,	Sept. 16, "
Robert L. Grier,	Sept. 6, "	Miss Dowlin,	" 16, "
Ann Thompson,	" 10, "	Andrew Torbet,	Nov. 25, "
Child of C. Guiney,	" 19, "	Child of John Dorlan,	Dec. 24, "
Sarah Atkins,	" 24, "	Robert Graham,	Jan. 4, 1861.
Sarah Miller,	" 25, "	James M'Clure,	" 8, "
Joseph Townsly,	Oct. 14, "	George McKim,	" 10, "
Joseph Smith,	Nov. 3, "	Jane Jenkins,	Feb. 11, "
Hannah Jackson,	" 20, "	Child of J. Essick,	" 16, "
Margaret Worrall,	" 30, "	Isaac Long,	" 18, "

APPENDIX.

Name.	Date of Burial.	Name.	Date of Burial.
Sarah Murdock,	Feb. 21, 1861.	Marshall Weber,	Mar. 19, 1862.
Emana McConnel,	" 26, "	Child of William Boyce,	April 1, "
Mrs. J. McCurdy,	Mar. 15, "	Mary Ann Walker,	May 18, "
Child of John Hughes,	" 25, "	Huldah Shields,	June 6, "
Ewing Lewis,	April 8, "	John Gallagher,	" 13, "
Mrs. Riddle,	" 8, "	Two children of T. Mc-	
Martha Gaston,	May 24, "	Adams,	" 20, "
William Himmelwright,	June 6, "	William N. Long,	July 14, "
Sarah West,	Aug. 9, "	Jane Roseborough,	" 21, "
Margaret McClure,	" 12, "	Child of J. Dunn,	" 21, "
—— Torbit,	" 14, "	Susannah Criley,	" 25, "
William Sterrett,	Sept. 25, "	Child of J. Danman,	Aug. 9, "
Child of T. McAdams,	Oct. 1, "	Child of John Clour,	Sept. 4, "
Nancy Crowe,	" 21, "	Margaret Lomas,	" 8, "
Philip B. Umstead,	" 22, "	James Murdock,	" 8, "
Hannah Seeright,	" 28, "	Child of Wm. Dowlin,	" 12, "
Sallie Hatfield,	Nov. 11, "	Child of Geo. Dowlin,	" 19, "
Son of B. Hatfield,	" 12, "	Ida McFarlane,	" 29, "
Child of B. Hatfield,	Dec. 1, "	James Sims,	" 30, "
Jane Butler,	" 2, "	Child of S. Mendenhall,	Dec. 10, "
Child of J. G. McClure,	" 10, "	James Lewis,	Jan. 8, 1863.
William Stanly,	" 12, "	Andrew Hatfield,	" 22, "
James Lockhart,	" 12, "	Robert Ralston,	Feb. 10, "
Child of J. Rice,	" 24, "	John Clower,	" 26, "
Child of B. Stringfellow,	" 31, "	Frank Ballentine,	Mar. 1, "
Joseph Lomas,	Jan. 12, 1862.	Jane Allan,	" 4, "
Michael Weber,	" 25, "	John C. Marshall,	" 15, "
Sarah Williams,	Mar. 3, "	Samuel Mowdy,	" 26, "
Child of E. Dunwoody,	" 12, "		

NAMES OF THOSE BURIED IN THE GRAVEYARDS BELONGING TO THE CHURCH, DURING NINE YEARS, MAY, 1876, TO MAY, 1885.

Name.	Date of Burial.	Name.	Date of Burial.
James McFarlan,	May 1, 1876.	Grier Davis,	Dec. 20, 1876.
Sonnoethon Essick,	" 3, "	Eber Thompson,	Jan. 9, 1877.
Minnie Witte,	" 22, "	Child of David Bruner,	" 17, "
Rebecca Mowdy,	June 20, "	Jane Guiney,	Feb. 20, "
Jane Long,	Sept. 7, "	Margaret White,	April 4, "
Rebecca Pinkerton,	" 14, "	Rachel Templeton,	" 20, "
William C. Lewis,	Oct. 6, "	Harry J. McLaughlin,	May 21, "
Norris Dowlin,	" 7, "	Esther M. Sinn,	June 8, "
George Guiney,	" 9, "	Lydia M. Thomas,	" 26, "
Mary Davidson,	Nov. 6, "	Child of Wm. Carpenter,	Aug. 7, "
John Kurtz,	Dec. 4, "	Elizabeth Guiney,	" 14, "
Emma Saylor,	" 9, "	Child of George Ayres,	" 24, "

APPENDIX.

Name.	Date of Burial.	Name.	Date of Burial.
Eliza Grove,	Oct. 1, 1877.	Anna L. Amole,	Dec. 22, 1879.
Frances Dowlin,	" 1, "	Agnes Happersett,	" 27, "
Eliza Lightfoot,	Nov. 8, "	Zaccheus H. Davis,	Jan. 26, 1880.
Sarah A. Pinkerton,	Dec. 20, "	Margaret A. Strong,	" 29, "
Child of J. M. Barr.		Elizabeth Christman,	Feb. 21, "
Isaac Williams,	" 27, "	Joseph Mackelduff, Jr.,	Mar. 2, "
Emma Long,	Jan. 31, 1878.	Peter Kurtz,	" 20, "
Elizabeth Gallagher,	Feb. 7, "	Ann Kennedy,	" 24, "
Howard C. Matlack,	Mar. 4, "	Harry Dowlin,	" 27, "
Jennie Ayres,	" 7, "	John Ralston,	April 25, "
Joseph Tregoe,	" 15, "	Harry Rea,	May 26, "
Yearsly C. Matlack,	" 16, "	James C. Irwin,	" 31, "
Charles Matlack,	" 22, "	Esther Kirkpatrick,	June 15, "
Mary J. Matlack,	May 6, "	Emma Millegan,	" 23, "
Benjamin Hatfield,	" 28, "	David Long,	July 2, "
Elizabeth Moore,	June 1, "	Frank Guthrie,	" 8, "
Elizabeth Christy,	" 29, "	Elizabeth Hatfield,	Aug. 12, "
Eva M. Granger,	July 14, "	Cephas M'Clune,	" 18, "
John Hughes,	Sept. 5, "	Rev. Dr. J. N. C. Grier,	Sept. 15, "
Margaret Hunter,	" 5, "	Nathaniel Irwin,	" 29, "
Samuel Forbis,	" 7, "	Sharpless Widener,	Oct. 11, "
John Reibeling,	Oct. 3, "	Christiana Crowe,	" 19, "
Mary A. Swinehart,	" 4, "	Fannie Lewis,	Nov. 17, "
John Criley,	" 9, "	Esther J. Baldwin,	Dec. 31, "
Mary R. Davis,	" 18, "	James McClure,	Jan. 18, 1881.
John Dowlin,	Nov. 9, "	Sarah Linden,	" 19, "
Charles Gillespie,	" 9, "	Mary Matlack,	Feb. 19, "
Mary Gallagher,	" 26, "	Joseph G. Maitland,	Mar. 19, "
Margaret Martin,	Dec. 10, "	Esther A. West,	" 26, "
Anna E. Ballentine,	" 15, "	William Templeton,	April 27, "
William Ballentine,	Jan. 24, 1879.	James Brown,	May 4, "
John Sailor,	Mar. 14, "	John Carpenter,	" 14, "
Mary Stringfellow,	" 31, "	Sarah Miller,	June 14, "
George Marshall,	April 8, "	A. M. Eachus,	Aug. 9, "
Robert Murduck,	" 11, "	James M. Dorlan,	Sept. 2, "
Child of John Guthrie,	" 19, "	Louisa Rea,	" 21, "
William Hammond,	May 3, "	Catharine Crowe,	" 28, "
Margaret Sailer,	July 3, "	Daniel Shields,	Nov. 12, "
Maria McGlaughlin,	Aug. 2, "	Rachel Everhart,	Dec. 1, "
William C. Long,	" 31, "	Mary Lewis,	" 28, "
Isaac Graham,	Sept. 15, "	Daniel McKim,	" 31, "
Alexander Wilson,	" 22, "	Lydia E. Thomas,	Jan. 12, 1882.
James Gallagher,	" 23, "	Elizabeth Umstead,	" 14, "
Child of Wm. Tregoe,	Oct. 1, "	Sarah A. Thompson,	" 28, "
Mary Dowlin,	Nov. 18, "	Tilla R. Forbis,	Mar. 10, "
Child of Dr. H. Evans,	Dec. 1, "	Annie E. Moore,	" 25, "
Ella Hatfield,	" 11, "	Catharine J. Forbis,	April 19, "

APPENDIX.

Name.	Date of Burial.	Name.	Date of Burial.
Child of F. H. Irwin,	May 12, 1882.	Emma A. Vance,	Dec. 11, 1883.
Mary Ann Grier,	June 8, "	Christiana Ralston,	Jan. 2, 1884.
Benjamin Milnes,	" 10, "	John Guthrie,	" 9, "
Savilla Hatfield,	" 20, "	Lewis V. Reeser,	" 17, "
Zillah Robinson,	July 1, "	James Davidson,	" 19, "
Alexander Martin,	" 4, "	George Cain,	Feb. 2, "
Ann E. Malin,	Aug. 18, "	Eugene Dowlin,	" 26, "
Anna K. Clower,	" 21, "	Agnes Himmelwright,	Mar. 22, "
Daniel Harris,	Sept. 9, "	Rebecca Robinson,	" 23, "
A. H. Umstead,	" 16, "	Thomas McAdams,	April 5, "
Thomas J. Dorlan,	Oct. 24, "	James Ballentine,	" 12, "
Liza M. Nelson,	Nov. 1, "	Moses Emery,	" 14, "
James Roseboro,	" 10, "	Susan Hammond,	" 27, "
John Guiney,	Dec. 13, "	Augustus J. Dowlin,	May 22, "
Dr. A. K. Gaston,	" 26, "	Eliza A. M'Clune,	" 28, "
Elizabeth Guiney,	Feb. 13, 1883.	Rebecca Dorlan,	June 4, "
Mary J. Graham,	" 19, "	Harriet Thompson,	July 4, "
John Dunn,	" 22, "	Samuel Mackelduff,	Aug. 2, "
Susan Liggett,	Mar. 1, "	John M. Neely,	" 8, "
Mary Carr,	" 11, "	Rachel Buchanan,	" 9, "
Esther J. Pinkerton,	May 16, "	Lizzie McFarlane,	Oct. 26, "
Joseph Briggs,	" 9, "	Robert Neely,	Nov. 5, "
Thomas Lomas,	" 15, "	Mrs. Maitland,	" 10, "
Benjamin McClure,	June 14, "	Ann Worrall,	Dec. 6, "
Elizabeth Gillespie,	July 16, "	Mary Clevenstine,	" 23, "
James Stewart,	" 29, "	William Moore,	Jan. 9, 1885.
Mary H. Dunwoody,	Aug. 1, "	Sarah Hatfield,	Mar. 10, "
Catharine Guiney,	" 9, "	James Grant,	April 1, "
Hannah McIntyre,	" 16, "	Sarah H. Gillespie,	" 3, "
Ethel M. McGlaughlin,	Sept. 15, "	E. H. Melon,	" 7, "
Harvey Milligan,	" 16, "	Anna M. F. Reaser,	" 9, "
Child of John Baldwin,	" 18, "	Emerson Matlack,	" 22, "
Mary M. Dowlin,	" 25, "	Charles McFarlane,	May 4, "
William Growe,	" 25, "	James G. Templeton,	" 9, "
William Lightfoot,	Oct. 22, "	James Ralston, Sr.,	" 22, "
Eddie Guiney,	Dec. 1, "	Alexander Morrison,	" 26, "
Child of Charles Ahmole,	" 8, "		

The above list includes every age, from the infant of "a few days" to the "mother in Israel" of more than fourscore and ten.

It is worthy of remark, as showing the healthfulness of the surrounding country, that more than one-eighth had reached ages varying from seventy to ninety-one years.

S.

ACT OF INCORPORATION.

ACT TO INCORPORATE THE PRESBYTERIAN CONGREGATION OF BRANDYWINE, IN THE TOWNSHIP OF WEST NANTMEAL, IN THE COUNTY OF CHESTER.

SECTION 1.—WHEREAS, divers members of the Presbyterian Congregation of Brandywine, in the township of West Nantmeal, in the County of Chester, have humbly petitioned the General Assembly, praying that the said Congregation may be incorporated, and thereby enabled to recover, receive, and hold bequests, legacies and donations which may be made to the use of the same Congregation, and that Samuel Cunningham, John Culbertson, Nathaniel Porter, Robert Smith, David Denny, Robert Lockhart, James Dunwoody, James M'Clure and Wm. Anderson, members of the aforesaid Congregation, may be constituted the first Trustees by Act of General Assembly, to be passed for that purpose.

And whereas, this General Assembly hath consented that the same Congregation be incorporated, and vested with such powers and privileges, as have been heretofore granted to other religious societies which have been incorporated by acts of the Legislature: Therefore,

SECTION 2.—Be it enacted, and it is hereby enacted by the Representatives of the Freemen of the Commonwealth of Pennsylvania in General Assembly met, and by the authority of the same, That the said Samuel Cunningham, John Culbertson, Nathaniel Porter, Robert Smith, David Denny, Robert Lockhart, James Dunwoody, James M'Clure and William Anderson, and their successors, to be nine in number, and to be duly elected as hereinafter is directed, be, and they are hereby made and constituted one body politic and corporate in law and in fact, to have continuance forever, by the name, style and title of "The Trustees of the Presbyterian Congregation of Brandywine, in the township of West Nantmeal, in the county of Chester."

SECTION 3.—And be it further enacted by the authority aforesaid, That the said Trustees and their successors, by the name, style and title aforesaid, shall forever hereafter be capable in law, as well to take, receive and hold all and all manners of lands and other real and personal estate, which have at any time or times heretofore been granted, bargained, sold, enfeoffed, released, devised or otherwise given, granted or bequeathed to the said religious society and congregation of Brandywine, in the county of Chester, or to any person or persons in trust for the said society and congregation. And the said Trustees and their successors, are hereby declared to be seized and possessed of such estate therein, and for the same uses and intents, as in and by the respective grant, devise or other instrument is set forth and limited. And moreover, the said Trustees and their successors, at all times hereafter, shall be able and capable to purchase, take, hold and enjoy for the use of the said Congregation, any real estate in fee simple or less estate, by gift, grant, alienation, devise or other act or instrument, of and from any person capable to make the same. And further, the same Trustees and their successors, shall apply the rents, profits and yearly income of the said Congregation, for the time being, for repairing and enlarging, if need be, the house of public worship and the enclosure of the burying ground of the same, and to erect and repair the schoolhouse,' and for such other pious and charitable purposes, as shall be directed by the major vote of the regular members of the said society and congregation duly assembled, upon public notice thereof the Sunday preceding, from the pulpit or desk of the said house of worship.

SECTION 4.—Be it further enacted by the authority aforesaid, That all and singular the powers, privileges, regulations, provisions and directions, subject to the limitations and restrictions contained in an Act of the General Assembly, entitled " An Act for incorporating the Presbyterian Congregation of Pequea, in the county of Lancaster," enacted on the fifth day of February, in the year of our Lord one thousand seven hundred and eighty-five, mutatis mutandis, shall be, and the same are hereby extended and applied to the said Congregation of Brandywine and to the nine Trustees herein before mentioned, and their successors:

SECTION 5.—Provided, nevertheless, That no sale or alienation of the real estate of the said Corporation, made by the said Trustees or their successors, bona fide and for valuable consideration, in case the possession thereof pass immediately to the purchaser thereof and continue in him or his assigns, shall be impeached or called in question, for want of the consent of the majority of the regular members of the said society and congregation, given as required by the Act aforesaid, unless the same be done within seven years from and after the sale and delivery of possession to the said purchaser.

Signed by order of the House.

THOMAS MIFFLIN, *Speaker.*

Enacted into a law at Philadelphia, on Friday, the first day of September, in the year of our Lord, one thousand seven hundred and eighty-six.

SAMUEL BRYAN, *Clerk of the General Assembly.*

A true copy from the original, by

B. GRIFFITH.

January 14, 1831.

ACT FOR INCORPORATING THE PRESBYTERIAN CONGREGATION OF PEQUEA, IN THE TOWNSHIP OF SALISBURY AND COUNTY OF LANCASTER.

SECTION 1.—WHEREAS, the Presbyterian Congregation of Pequea, in the county of Lancaster, have prayed that their said Congregation may be incorporated, and by law enabled as a body corporate and politic, to receive and hold such charitable donations and bequests as have been, or that hereafter may be made to their society, and vested with such powers and privileges as are enjoyed by other religious societies, who are incorporated within this State. And whereas, this house is disposed to exercise the powers vested in the Legislature of the Commonwealth for the encouragement of pious and charitable purposes:

SECTION 2.—Be it therefore enacted, and it is hereby enacted by the Representatives of the Freemen of the Commonwealth of Pennsylvania, in General Assembly met, and by the authority of the same, That Isaac M'Calmont, Amos Slaymaker, James Armour, Thomas Slemons, Andrew Caldwell, Robert Byers, David Jenkins, Thomas Patton and the Rev. Robert Smith, and their successors duly elected and appointed in such manner as herein after is directed, be, and they are hereby made and constituted a corporation and body politic, in law and in fact, to have continuance forever, by the name, style and title of "The Trustees of the Presbyterian Congregation of Pequea, in Salisbury township and county of Lancaster."

SECTION 3.—And be it further enacted by the authority aforesaid, That the said corporation and their successors, by the name, style and title aforesaid, shall forever hereafter be persons able and capable in law, as well to take, receive and hold, all and all manner of lands, tenements, rents, annuities, franchises and other hereditaments, which at any time or times heretofore have been granted, bargained, sold, enfeoffed, released, devised or otherwise conveyed to the said Presbyterian Congregation of Pequea, in the township and county aforesaid, or to the religious society or congregation worshipping therein, now under the pastoral care of the Rev. Robert Smith, or to any person or persons to their use or in trust for them; and the same lands, tenements, rents, annuities, liberties, franchises and other hereditaments are hereby vested and established in the said corporation and their successors forever, according to the original use and intent, for which such devices, gifts and grants were respectively made: And the said corporation and their successors are hereby declared to be seized and possessed of such estate and estates therein as in and by the respective grants, bargains, sales, enfeoffments, releases, devises, or other conveyances thereof, is, or are declared, limited or expressed: As also that the said corporation and their successors aforesaid, at all times hereafter, shall be capable and able to purchase, have, receive, take, hold and enjoy, in fee simple, or of lesser estate or estates, any lands, tenements, rents, annuities, liberties, franchises and other hereditaments, by the gift, grant, bargain, sale, alienation, enfeoffment, release, confirmation or devise of any person or persons, bodies politic and corporate, capable and able to make the same: And further that the said corporation may take and receive any sum or sums of money, and any portion of goods and chattels, that have been or hereafter shall be given or bequeathed to them by any person or persons, bodies corporate and politic, able and capable to make a bequest or gift thereof, such money, goods and chattels to be laid out and disposed of for the use and benefit of the aforesaid Congregation, agreeable to the intention of the donor.

SECTION 4.—Be it further enacted by the authority aforesaid, That the rents, profits and interest of the said real and personal estate of the aforesaid corporation and congregation, shall by the said Trustees and their successors, from time to time, be applied and laid out by them for the maintainance and support of the Gospel Ministry in the said congregation, for repairing and maintaining their house of public worship, lots of land, burial ground, and such other pious and charitable uses as shall be thought proper, by a majority of the Trustees and other regular members of the said congregation, on due notice met, to give their free vote in such case.

SECTION 5.—Be it further enacted by the authority aforesaid, That when and as often as it may become necessary to rebuild, enlarge or otherwise alter the house of public worship belonging to the said congregation and corporation, or to erect any new building, or to make any new purchase for the use of the said congregation, then and in such case it may be lawful for the aforesaid Trustees and their successors to make sale of such part or parcel of the real or personal estate of the said corporation, as a majority of the Trustees and of the regular members of the said congregation shall by their votes direct, the money arising from such sale to be laid out and applied, agreeably to the vote of a majority met as aforesaid.

SECTION 6.—Be it further enacted by the authority aforesaid, That the said Trustees and their successors shall not by deed nor any otherwise grant, alien, convey, or otherwise dispose of any part or parcel of the estate, real or personal, in the said corporation vested, or to be vested, or charge or incumber the same to any person or persons whatsoever, except in the manner and for the purposes herein before mentioned.

SECTION 7.—Be it further enacted by the authority aforesaid, That the said Trustees, their successors, or a majority of them, may from time to time meet as often as they shall think necessary for the benefit of the said corporation, either on their own adjournment, or on public notice from the pulpit the preceding Sabbath immediately after divine service, and before the congregation is dismissed, or on regular notice in writing, left at the house of each of the Trustees, and that the said Trustees, or a majority of them, being so met, be authorized and empowered, and they are hereby authorized and empowered to elect and appoint from among themselves a President, and also to elect and appoint from among themselves, or other members of the said congregation, a Treasurer and Secretary, and to remove, change or continue all or either of them at their pleasure, as shall seem to be most for the benefit of the said corporation.

SECTION 8.—Provided, nevertheless, That the meeting or meetings of the said corporation be not called without the concurrence of two or more Trustees, or of three or more respectable members of the said congregation, with the President, or without the particular business and reasons of the meeting being specified with the notification.

SECTION 9.—Be it further enacted by the authority aforesaid, That the said Trustees, or a majority of them, met, as is herein before directed, shall be authorised and empowered, and they are hereby authorised and empowered, to make rules, by-laws and ordinances, and to do every thing needful for the government and support of the secular affairs of the said corporation and congregation: Provided that the said by-laws, rules and ordinances, or any of them, be not repugnant to the laws of this commonwealth; and also that all their laws and proceedings be fairly and regularly entered in a book to be kept for that purpose.

SECTION 10.—Be it further enacted by the authority aforesaid, That the said corporation and their successors shall have full power and authority to make, have and use one common seal, with such device and inscription as they shall think fit and proper, and the same to break, alter and renew at their pleasure.

SECTION 11.—Be it further enacted by the authority aforesaid, That the said corporation and their successors, by the name of "The Trustees of the Presbyterian Congregation of Pequea, in the township of Salisbury and county of Lancaster," shall be able and capable in law to sue and be sued, plead and be impleaded in any Court, or before any Judge or Justice, in all and all manner of suits, complaints, pleas, matters and demands of whatsoever kind, nature or form they may be, and all and every matter and thing therein to do, in as full and effectual a manner as any other person or persons, bodies politic or corporate, within this Commonwealth, may or can do.

SECTION 12.—Be it further enacted by the authority aforesaid, That the said corporation shall always consist of nine members, except as is herein after provided, called and known by the name of "The Trustees of the Presbyterian Congregation of Pequea, in the township of Salisbury, and county of Lancaster," and the said members shall at all times hereafter be chosen by ballot by a majority of such members (met together) of the said congregation as shall have been enrolled as stated worshippers with the said congregation for at least the space of one year, and shall have paid one year's pew rent, or other annual sum of money not less than ten shillings, for the use and benefit of the said corporation and congregation, and shall not at any time of voting, be more than one half year behind or in arrears for the same: Provided, always, that the Pastor or Minister of the said congregation for the time being, shall be entitled to vote equally with any member of the said congregation, and also, that all and every person or persons qualified to vote and elect as aforesaid, shall and may be also capable of being elected as a Trustee as aforesaid.

SECTION 13.—Be it enacted by the authority aforesaid, That the said Isaac M'Calmont, Amos Slaymaker, James Armour, Thomas Slemons, Andrew Caldwell, Robert Byers, David Jenkins, Thomas Patton, and the Rev. Robert Smith, the first and present Trustees hereby incorporated, shall be and continue Trustees aforesaid, until they be removed in manner following, that is to say: One third part in number of the Trustees aforesaid, being the third part herein first named and appointed, shall cease and discontinue, and their appointment determine on the first Monday in the month of April, which will be in the year of our Lord one thousand seven hundred and eighty-six, and the second third part herein named shall cease and discontinue, and their appointment determine on the first Monday in April, which will be in the year one thousand seven hundred and eighty-seven, and in like manner the last third part herein named shall cease and determine on the first Monday in April, which will be in the year one thousand seven hundred and eighty-eight, on which days in each of the aforementioned years respectively, new elections shall be held of other Trustees, instead and in place of those whose appointments shall have ceased and terminated; which manner of discontinuance, determination and new appointment or election shall be continued on the first Monday in April every year hereafter forever, so that no person shall be or continue a Trustee longer than three years together, without being re-elected, which may be done whenever and as often as the members of said congregation qualified to vote as aforesaid, shall think fit.

SECTION 14.—Provided, always, nevertheless, That whenever any circumstance or concurrence of circumstances shall happen, to prevent the holding of an election at the periods aforementioned, for Trustees instead and in place of those whose appointments shall have ceased and terminated, also whenever any vacancy shall happen by the death, refusal to serve, or other removal of any one or more of the Trustees of the said corporation, an election shall be held as soon as conveniently can be done, in the manner before directed, for other Trustees in the stead and in place of those whose appointments shall have ceased and terminated, or for supplying such vacancies that may happen as aforesaid, and that the remaining Trustees have power to call a meeting of the electors of the Congregation for such purposes.

SECTION 15.—Provided, always, and it is hereby enacted by the authority aforesaid, That the clear yearly value, interest or income of the lands, tenements, rents, annuities, or other hereditaments and real estate of the said Corporation, shall not exceed the sum of five hundred pounds, gold or silver money, at the present current value thereof in the Commonwealth of Pennsylvania, exclusive of pew rent and other free contributions belonging to the aforesaid congregation, which said money shall be received by the said Trustees, and disposed of by them for the purposes and in manner herein before described and directed.

Signed by order of the House.

JOHN BAYARD, *Speaker.*

Enacted into a law at Philadelphia on Saturday the fifth day of February, in the year of our Lord one thousand seven hundred and eighty-five.

SAMUEL BRYAN, *Clerk of the General Assembly.*

A true copy from the original, by
B. GRIFFITH.
January 14, 1831.

www.ingramcontent.com/pod-product-compliance
Lightning Source LLC
Chambersburg PA
CBHW031943230426
43672CB00010B/2038